"*Fairly Smooth Operator* is a book of unpredictable adventures and unbelievable truths. The author's relatable, unique tell-all is a story for veterans, especially female veterans, and women alike. Her story is inspiring and truly empowering."

—DANIEL "DOC" JACOBS, recipient of Bronze Star with Valor, Purple Heart, and author of *There and Back Again: Stories from a Combat Navy Corpsman*

"You have in your hands a carefully crafted book that tells a unique life experience full of wisdom, wit, and grit. Caroline Walsh takes you on a ride into her personal life experience that is not only raw but one that I found myself thinking and laughing at the same time as I read her life story. She makes serious issues easy to read by how she paints her life experiences in her own words, way, and style, leaving you wanting to know more."

—PEARL GIFTY ALIMO, author of *Growing Your Family: Learn How To Flourish and Thrive as a Military Family*

"Just like Christopher Walken needs more cowbell, we need stories of women in the Coast Guard. Caroline tells her story with humor and grace. As a fellow veteran, I found myself chuckling out loud at her descriptions of the people and culture unique to the military. She is also courageous enough to speak about the racism and harassment that many experience in service. I would promise myself, 'just one more page,' and then an hour later found myself wondering what happened to the time."

—MAUREEN ELIAS, US Army veteran and military spouse

Fairly Smooth Operator:
My Life Occasionally at the Tip of the Spear

by Caroline Walsh

Published by

◄ köehlerbooks™

3705 Shore Drive
Virginia Beach, VA 23455
800-435-4811
www.koehlerbooks.com

fairly

SMOOTH OPERATOR

MY LIFE OCCASIONALLY
AT THE TIP OF THE SPEAR

CAROLINE WALSH

VIRGINIA BEACH
CAPE CHARLES

tip of the spear

An American idiom commonly used in military operations to mean the first soldiers to go into a war zone. In common usage it means the first to venture into a new endeavor.

—Urban Dictionary

TABLE OF CONTENTS

PROLOGUE

FAIRLY SMOOTH OPERATOR WAS produced after creating and performing a five-minute comedy set, facilitated by the Armed Service Arts Partnership. I realized through the laughs that there was more to the story of developing as a young woman in military and government organizations, especially following confusing war premises and a global financial crisis. The stories in this book expand on mostly inappropriate or depressing situations. They involve real ocean waves, real ocean creatures, and waves of emotion that come along with being lost, finding your direction, ruling out not what is not your direction, and accepting that you may just be the kind of person who is always lost.

There are disgruntled moments that are mostly part of growing up and figuring out how to maintain a balance between control and faith. Finding the balance between those two forces can be especially difficult when in a military organization that takes away most of your control yet doesn't give you a lot in which you can put your faith.

Fairly Smooth Operator is based on actual events. Some are more ridiculous than can even be described in words. Most names have been changed and some characters have been fused to protect the identities of the greatest and the not-the-greatest people I encountered through my time in the Coast Guard and the CIA.

The point of the book is primarily to entertain readers who can relate to these cultures and provide comedic insight for readers who do not yet know the ridiculousness of being young and navigating historic US organizations. These are groups that are only lately making room for a representative percentage of leaders who are not White and male. That being said, I am White. My family is made up of half Irish academics, whose ancestors snuck across the Canadian border to work in Montana's coal mines, and half Polish Libertarians, who would rather be living on farmland and setting off fireworks than functioning in any form of society. Not that being White makes everything easy, but along with focus and hard work, I am sure there are instances in which I received the benefit of the doubt—despite my antics—that allowed me to get to where I am.

A big thanks to the United States of America whose ongoing struggle with interpreting and protecting freedom has given me the privilege to talk shit about whatever I want. As long as I'm not revealing secrets (go to hell, Snowden), I can publish it all for the public to engage with, without fear of jail time or harm to my family (what's up, China and Russia?). Also, a shout out to the Coast Guard. Even though my experience with the organization included many unnecessary challenges, I have a lot of respect for the people who are out there securing the coastline, enjoying the waves, and shining the light to improve its dark spots. The same respect goes to the CIA, but they don't need to be told they are awesome.

CHAPTER 1

HOW TO LOSE YOUR STARTING POSITION

I can't stand motivational posters that say
that failure is not an option because it definitely is.

"YOU WANT SOME TEA?" he asked as the smoke cleared enough to make squinty eye contact with me through the haze.

We were sitting in the military barracks that had been renovated into dorm rooms at the old Fort Ord Army base, now California State University Monterey Bay (CSUMB). The room was engulfed in incense, fresh weed, and now tea that was brewing. It was Friday night and the school campus, scattered with abandoned buildings, including military airplane hangars left over from its time as a base during WWII, was calling to be explored.

A soccer scholarship brought me from the suburbs of Cleveland, Ohio to Monterey, California. I was born in Riverside (909) and then, thanks to my Ohio-bred mother and father from San Diego who went with the flow, I spent most of my childhood living outside of Cleveland, enjoying summertime trips to the Outer Banks coastal waters to surf, but otherwise remaining painfully immersed in the conservative, small Midwest town's judgment.

I was athletic, though, and soccer was my way out; even with my dad never taking any videos or pushing too hard, I managed to scavenge a few videos of my high school games to catch the attention of the Monterey coach. That was thanks to a friend's helicopter dad who videotaped every game and was kind and dedicated enough to sort out clips of me to send around to colleges.

As a freshman at CSUMB, I started every soccer game, but the team struggled, and I soon became indifferent to the glory of being *that starting freshman*. It didn't help that the weed in Monterey was strong, and with it, my dedication to the team slowly deteriorated.

"Let's go," one guy said, and they all made movements to grab their skateboards.

"Let me get my bike," I replied, as I was about to make my way down the hall to grab my beach cruiser.

I put my hand out to reach the doorknob to exit but was cut off by a longboard—a cruising skateboard made out of flexible bamboo— shoved in front of me.

"Nah, you're riding this," Charlie said and gave me a warm smile that radiated so much confidence, I absorbed some of it for myself. It was a look and an energy that removed any opportunity for me to object.

Charlie gave me a quick lesson in the flat parking lot as the other guys practiced their tricks. The air echoed with the distinctive clacking sound that a skateboard makes when it hits the curb. Before I was aware, we had started skating out of the parking lot and were off on the adventure through the dark paved paths of the campus.

I trailed behind, slowing on the big hills, getting a feel for the board. As things picked up, we moved liked a pack through the campus, skating upon the abandoned military base roads that led to nowhere and on new campus roads that led to low-key night life. We came across a small concert hall where a band was playing, listened to a song, and then left the crowd for more cruising and thought-provoking silence. With ease, we stopped and grouped up throughout the ride, like water slowing through a narrow pathway and then releasing again. While paused, we'd look up at the stars or wait for someone to decide which fork in the road to take next. The hills grew, and so did my skills; like a child learning a language, I was picking it up without realizing it. Smoothly cruising now, I could breathe in the cool night air and exaggerate my turns through the judgment-free darkness.

By midnight, we had ventured for miles and made it back to the dimly lit quad where a sidewalk path connected the dorm room buildings. It was a final meetup before we parted ways. I had a soccer game the next day, home turf ten o'clock, which would give me plenty of time to sleep and let the blurry high slowly release itself as my brain continued to skateboard through my dreams. While saying our goodbyes, I had one foot on the board and one on the pavement. I made a small motion to adjust my stance and *crack*! I lost my balance. My foot bent under me, twisting my right ankle.

Charlie caught me as I tried to step down and in the haze of pain, I realized the damage I had just done. I leaned on him, and he grabbed the bamboo board, helping me hobble back to my room.

The next morning, my ankle was swollen. I had sprained it a year before and in comparison, knew that this one was bad. I didn't want the team's athletic trainer to know. She was kind of a bitch, and overly controlling of the players. I sat in bed and taped it myself, layers and layers of white athletic tape to try to keep the swelling down and my ankle in place. With pride at my self-sufficiency and an air of mischievousness for dodging the trainer, I put on my soccer socks to hide my handiwork, grabbed my soccer bag and walked down the stairs, testing it out with a hesitant limp.

I made it to the first landing on the stairs and ran into Charlie coming back from breakfast. I told him my ankle wasn't good and he reached in his pocket and pulled out a black and gray film canister. He opened the bottle, tilted it, and tapped out two tablets into his palm to offer me. I took the pills from his hand and swallowed them with a sip of my Gatorade.

"Thanks," I said.

"See you at the game," he replied.

During warmups I found I could jog and forget the pain, for the most part. If I got through this game, I would be able to recover next week during practice, maybe see the trainer as if the injured condition had just happened.

I started in my usual left defensive position. Before the whistle blew, I looked over to the stands and saw the same group of guys from last night's skating adventures. They were filtering into the stands, wearing trucker hats and dark sunglasses to shield the morning sun. I felt one of those sparks of happiness that makes you smile without realizing it. How nice that they made the effort to wake up in time to come out—even if they were only here to check out the rest of the women on the team.

The plays went on and I wasn't in too much pain. The warm happiness stayed with me, but the field began to feel different. My teammates sounded distant, my movements felt smooth but delayed. The ball went out and someone called my name.

"Walsh!" she yelled and waved me in as she jogged toward me. I was being subbed out. Replaced for the first time that season.

I got to the bench and didn't get much of an explanation from the coach. Still in my own world, I grabbed my water and leaned back to watch; the sun felt nice on my skin. Although my replacement wasn't better than me, she was likely better than the version of myself that was now obviously high and sporting a sprained ankle.

I eventually exposed my mummified ankle so the trainer could apply ice and elevate. She tried to shame me for not seeing her earlier.

"You have trainers for a reason. You shouldn't be playing with your ankle like this."

Exactly, you wouldn't have let me play.

In my slow and mellow speech, I waved off her criticism and mumbled something about being in a rush this morning. After the game, I got a ride back to the dorm, showered, and slept through the afternoon. By evening there was a knock at the door.

"How are you doing?" Charlie asked as he opened the door. I shrugged. I could feel myself not caring anymore—even less than usual. I gestured for him to come in. He sat down at my desk, pulled out a bowl, and filled it with fresh Humboldt weed.

After a few hits in comfortable silence, we went to get dinner, sitting down with the group from last night. They had also completed their pre-dinner toke ritual but were now riled up, finally awake for the evening. The sun was setting, and their amped-up energy helped to dissipate the melancholy I had been feeling.

"Dude, good game, but honestly, as the first half went on, you started moving more and more slowly!" one guy mimed slow-motion running and laughed with such amusement that I had to smile and laugh at myself. Whatever this was, I felt so much better in their company than I did with the soccer team.

I had no idea what I was doing. My ankle healed. The semester continued and so did the adventures and skateboarding. A nice girl from across the hallway lent me her almost never used bamboo longboard, a nicer version of the one I rode the first night. I rode it so much I trashed the pristine grip tape on the top with dirt and shoe marks. I bought my own board only after I had returned hers, looking obviously used. I felt bad and I hoped she would appreciate that now it looked like she rode it, instead of hating me for tearing it up so badly.

The season ended in late fall and during the winter off season, I suffered from shin splints from sprinting on the treadmill over my Ohio winter break. Returning in January, I asked the coach if I could swim instead of our team's training in the gym. She allowed it, possibly beginning to give up on me. My first self-instructed swim training turned into smoking a bowl with my neighbor and then going swimming.

"My mouth is dry, but the rest of me is wet." Our stoner observations seemed very profound as we glided through the water, diving deep, then reaching the wall and coming up to share more thought discoveries.

The swimming sessions morphed into surf sessions in Santa Cruz, driving back with friends and making it to Spanish class where

I'd open a book to find it filled with sand or lean over to grab my pen and half the ocean would drain from my sinuses onto the floor. I somehow went from the girl from Ohio to the female Spicoli who managed good grades only because everyone else's were worse. I had a sort of freedom I had never had before. Maybe too much freedom.

After an unknown amount of time filled with swimming and surf antics, I forced myself to be confrontational and requested a midsemester meeting with the coaches to state that I would give up playing soccer with the team, acknowledging that I knew it meant I would also give up my scholarship. They expressed concern, but it seemed like they saw it coming.

I had fun with my freedom. I experimented. I ran to make up for not practicing soccer and kept up with surfing as well as pickup games at the gym. I got up early some mornings to be alone in the fog. I'd run to the top of the sand dunes, bouncing on top of Monterey's aloe-like ice plant that grew at the base of the dunes and propelled me forward with each step. Once at the top, I sat in the sand to stretch and wait for the fog to burn away. As it dissipated, I could see downtown Monterey to the south and more hills and dunes of the old military base to the north. I would take out a book from my backpack, look ahead at the ocean, and watch the air and ocean life wake up with the sunrise. Birds glided over the ocean in their formations, pods of dolphins playfully made their way to schools of fish, and whales popped up in the distance.

I'd spend half the day watching the world and avoiding it at the same time. I eventually abandoned the skateboard group for the most part (you can never really abandon anything at a small college). In general, I made messes of relationships, occasionally discovering I was apparently dating someone only after they shared that they were under the impression that they were dating me. We all were on our own trip.

I eventually got my act together, sobering myself up around twenty-one years old. I transferred to a small Cal State college in southern California—a school that didn't allow skateboarding on campus—whose Friday night excitement consisted of In-N-Out Burger food trucks on campus. It was a school that restricted my freedom but provided a good education with more focused classes and a clear degree path. It was pretty tame. Drinking and playing rec soccer, I made friends who surfed and were doing well in school.

By graduation year, the 2008 recession hit. I was working at a soccer club managing the office. My two girlfriends came by one day to tell me they ran into a Coast Guard recruiter while they were surfing in Ventura and they were going to join after graduation. They told me I should join too and asked if I wanted to go for a sunset surf session that night.

"I have to work," I said. I was on the schedule at the local soccer club to check in and out players for their evening games.

They shrugged and said something to the effect of "suit yourself," as they giddily made their way to the beach, knowing their decision to join the Coast Guard released the weight of career uncertainty that builds during last semesters of college.

A month later, after serious contemplation stemming from a psychology class about the destructive mental effects of the *rat race*—that is, our nine-to-five, work-obsessed society—I signed up for the Coast Guard. The 2008 financial crisis meant my undergraduate degree and limited work experience were not in demand. Besides the Coast Guard, my psychology degree provided the following options: make twenty thousand a year as a social worker, go into debt for a graduate school to which I had not yet applied, or inquire about the American Gladiator audition advertisement that I saw in posted in LA—apparently the '80s show was making a comeback. I could not wrap my head around how I would work an hourly job, pay rent, pay for health insurance, and save for school. It took a surf session with the recruiter to seal the deal.

"Your DoD identification card is going to be like an all- access pass to surf breaks around the country," he told me, as he handed me Coast Guard Nike track pants and some other sporty swag.

Not only did he turn out to be right, but when I was on vacation in Hawaii a few years later, I hit him up.

"You're going to want to try the North Shore today. Get out to the *Glass Doors* break between noon and three and you'll be golden. Probably east coast of the island tomorrow, but I'll let you know," he texted.

He was an aviation technician for a base in Honolulu and provided daily surf reports from his morning helicopter rides around the island.

The college escapades were gone from my life, but the trip was about to continue.

CHAPTER 2

BOOT CAMP

My friends and I thought Coast Guard boot camp would be like a military version of Baywatch. We would train on the beach, practice valiant ocean rescues, and learn advanced first aid. Turned out, the only thing Baywatch-like would be our cheap, ultrathin bathing suits that showed every crevice and nipple detail.

THE THREE WOMEN WHO signed up for this together in Ventura, California received tons of athletic swag from the recruiter, who took us surfing on base like he had some kind of backstage pass, which he kind of did. It was a tough return to reality when we found out that the Coast Guard was not sponsored by Billabong and pushups were not going to give us Pam Anderson physiques. We were about to have eight weeks of boot-camp nonsense led by three dudes of varying respectability.

Of the three company commanders (CCs) in charge of our group, one was mostly respectable. He was thin and had a Staten Island accent. He also had a genuineness to him, like he believed in what he was doing and wasn't going to torture you as long as you were learning. Another was halfway decent. The halfway decent one was a heavy and stout guy with dark features. His bushy eyebrows almost connected in the center. He reminded me of someone's libertarian uncle who you laugh with so that you don't upset him. The third was skinny and bald and took his Black-Sabbath-T-shirt-wearing teen rage and insecurities out on a group of eighteen-to-twenty-eight-year-olds. If it had been allowed, he would have left us for days in a room with heavy metal blasting like Guantanamo Bay detainees.

It was easy to analyze the three of them and the others as they took turns controlling a group of 150 young adults, like summer camp counselors rotating through their shifts.

My favorite CC was the Staten Island nice guy. He cared about your development, but he had to yell at you even for doing the right thing. If he didn't yell, the other CCs would think he was soft.

"*What did you two females do? This clothing layout is wrong, but you did it wrong together. What, did you* collaborate? *Did you find an answer close enough to the correct one when the correct one wasn't available and carry it out?*" he barked and then walked away, leaving us to acknowledge momentary success and be thankful he was in charge. The next day, one of the other brutish CCs was in charge. He threw our folded clothing in various directions, scattering them throughout the bunk room, "*You have thirty seconds to clean this up and get into formation!*"

Another time, I had misplaced my ball cap—an item that must be worn the moment your foot hits the ground outside or you are out of regulations, and in boot camp that means a lot of hell for you or for your group through collective punishment. While still in the barracks, we were called to formation.

I scrambled. "Grab that one!" a guy said to me, trying to help. He was short and a little chunky.

"It's not mine!"

"Who cares? Just take it and get outside!"

I grabbed it, briefly seeing the name written inside in Sharpie clearly said, *Thompson* and not *Walsh*.

We were in formation—four by ten assigned in order of height— when Thompson walked out. Capless.

"*Recruit. Where the hell is your cover?*" (in the Coast Guard, a hat is called a *cover*).

"*Sir*. I don't know, *sir!*"

The crazy-eyed skinny, baldheaded, raging CC looked out at us frozen in formation, "*Where the hell is Thompson's cover?*" he bellowed.

I made corner-eye contact with the kid who had told me to grab the cap. "What the fuck?" I mouthed to him. He gave me a mild shrug, so he didn't get caught moving.

"*Sir*. Seaman Recruit Walsh," I said, identifying myself. "I have Thompson's ball cap, *sir!*"

"*Walsh! Fall out and get over here!*"

I left the formation to walk over to him next to Thompson and in front of everyone. It was a summer morning in Cape May, New Jersey, and had I been able to look around, I would have seen bland concrete buildings with the East Coast sun rising behind them.

I handed over the ball cap and now I was *uncovered* and out of regulations—outside without my cap.

"*Well? Where the hell is your cover, Walsh?*"

"*Sir*! Seaman Recruit Walsh. Respectfully request to return inside for my ball cap." I mustered up some courage in my voice and tried not to let it quiver.

"*You have fifteen seconds to get your cap and get back out here!*"

I took off. I ran inside the building, and when I got inside the glass business-building-like door, I glanced back and saw that the CC was chasing me. I ran up the tan marble steps that wound around like a spiral staircase, now sprinting. *Finally some cardio,* I thought and then lost track of where I was and went up another flight. I missed my floor. On the next floor there was another class of recruits; one guy was on the floor doing pushups as he was getting yelled at by his CC, who was a female redhead with the nickname the *Red Dragon*. It was chaos, she was yelling at and him and he was counting his pushups while yelling that he would never repeat his infraction again and again.

I stopped, realizing I had gone too far. My CC had caught up to me and was screaming, counting down fifteen seconds.

The Red Dragon looked at me with her piercing blue eyes that I was not supposed to look into. *"Who are you? You wanna do some pushups too, like Jacobson here? Get on the deck!"* She looked at my CC and he nodded at her, then he switched from counting down my time to screaming out how many pushups I was doing.

"Nineteen, twenty, Walsh! Dooone!," he barked. *"Now get your damn ball cap!"*

I flew down the stairs, now fully sweating before the day even started. I had no idea where my ball cap was located. I wasn't allowed to speak rationally to this man, so I frantically lifted mattresses as he watched and taunted me.

"You're running out of time, Walsh! Better check the bathroom hangers, Walsh!"

Ah fuck. I left it in the bathroom. I raced in and there it was, my dark blue ball cap with golden yellow Coast Guard writing.

"Better check that one is yours, Walsh! You steal another ball cap, you're outta here!"

I checked it. There it was, *WALSH* in black sharpie on the inner gray lining. *Steal? Really, did I steal? This guy was chasing me around to teach me a lesson about stealing? Maybe he needs a lesson on creating an environment open to conversation and conflict resolution. Besides, the short kid told me to do it. The lesson I learned is to not listen to that guy.*

I questioned the teaching philosophy of boot camp, which made me think that maybe I wasn't the kind of person who should be in this business. Giving me fifteen to thirty seconds to do something that everyone knows would take five to ten minutes didn't make me hurry, it made me confused about how much time I actually had to do this task. In incidents where I wasn't being chased, like having fifteen seconds to perfectly fold and place up my clothes that had been scattered around the room, I thought, *Okay I have fifteen seconds . . . should I do this whole task and take five minutes? Or should I just throw the clothes in my bunk as fast as I can and head out to formation?* Either way, I was going to be wrong. So, I became apathetic, which made boot camp easier. Maybe I *was* right for this line of work.

"*Walsh. Where do you think you are going*?"

"The wrong way, *sir*!"

It was the summer of 2009. Not only was swine flu was raging, but the economy had tanked six months earlier. It wasn't a bad time to be in a place where the only news of the week was the schedule of who had the midnight watch. Plus, I was making a salary for the first time in my life, an achievement other millennials who graduated college in this period would not experience until years later. So what if I had someone spit-yelling in my face?

Anyone who has seen any military movie knows that boot camp starts with getting off a bus and large men screaming in your face as you scramble to find out where you are supposed to be standing. I had never watched military movies, so this was all new to me. I had never even really been yelled at, which I'm not sure was a bad thing. I hadn't had someone an inch away from my face talking in a high volume, let alone screaming because my hair was in a ponytail and not a bun.

"*What the hell is this*?"

I tried to form words to ask what he was talking about, but there was too much commotion around me, with everyone getting yelled at for breaking rules that we didn't yet know. I froze with a look of confusion and fear, as if he realized that no words were going to form.

"*A ponytail is* not *authorized*!"

We made it to our bunks at last later that night. The room and bedding had a hue of 1970s yellow. I was on the top bunk, asking myself what I was doing here, when I saw the top of the company commander's tan hat coming my way. He was making the rounds through the bunk rooms. I thought that hat would continue to float past me, but it stopped, faced my bunk, and a giant ugly face with nighttime coffee breath was now an inch from me screaming:

"You watching me, Recruit? You will not *watch me. You making eye contact with me, Recruit? Don't look at me. You will sleep* now!"

I had a physical reaction to all of this angry yelling energy in my face, and in that moment on the top bunk, my body almost rid itself of everything in its digestive tract. I didn't know before that there was a literal reason for the phrase, *scare the shit out of you.* Would I fight this chaos or take flight? My body didn't care; it was preparing me for either.

As the yelling and alarms at unknown hours continued, their impact on my bodily systems lessened. Mid-training, I finally caught a real break. Swine flu. At the height of the pandemic, the pathological CC who would have rather been a prison guard took it upon himself to ramp up the spread.

"All of you. In!" he yelled at our company. His bald head shined, and his forehead scrunched as he yelled.

A few of us looked at him in disbelief as the others followed orders and marched into the steaming shower room that was supposed to hold maybe fifteen people. Soon there were fifty trainees in a steamy shower room, fully clothed—men and women—yelling something dumb continuously for half an hour. There was sweat and spit spewing everywhere. Our slimy arms touched each other as our elbows drooped from trying to hold our stupid fake rifles over our heads as we screamed.

"If I catch any of you only moving your mouths, you're done!" he barked, and we all continued to yell out of fear that we might fail boot camp for one incident of not yelling. In the moment, with our fears baked into our minds from weeks of discipline by adult men playing psychotic camp counselor, no one thought that maybe he was giving us a hint that we could take a break from yelling by only

moving our mouths. It didn't matter what he meant, though. I got the flu despite the possible hints and stringent protective measures against the H1N1 swine flu that the World Health Organization had warned was an imminent pandemic.

I spent four to five days in the sick ward. It smelled like a bucket of dirty mop water mixed with a few capfuls of bleach. I slept in stark white bedding and the floor was a cream-colored tile that had ashy blue and pink confetti glazed into it. There was nothing to do in the ward but stare at normal objects and try to make them interesting.

I wonder if the Coast Guard used the same tile contractor as my elementary school cafeteria for this speckled mosaic. Is that dust shining in the sun or silver speckles melted into the floor glistening?

In this location, we were all untouchable to the CCs. They even had to lower their voices in the sick ward area. I had a fevered dream that I was still a kid and was having a sick day at home from school. I dreamed I was laying on my childhood couch, a dark green wrap around, perfectly broken in. In my dream, I was watching "The Price in Right," but the sound was not working. "Mommm, this couch lost its cushion, why is it so uncomfortable now?" I yelled groggily to my imaginary mother. "Mommm what are you cleaning? It smells so bad, please stoppp. Mommm, it's really cold, can you bring me a real blanket, pleaaase? Where is the dog? I'm so cold." When I woke up my pillow was damp with sweat and instead of a dog, my only companion was the sleeping shipmate in the bunk to my right.

"You're back," I whispered to her when she finally woke up.

"*You're* back!" she replied, "You slept over ten hours today, I kept trying to ask you if you wanted to trade for my apple, but you were out cold. Sorry I ate it, but I think there will be more fresh fruit tomorrow."

I did my best to stay hydrated, but then regretted consuming all those liquids every time I had to make the exhausting walk across the cold tile floor to the bathroom. I was probably also exhausted because I was fed packaged lunches of a white-bread sandwich and canned peaches. I had just come from Los Angeles, where carbs were a big no-no, so I'd pick out the slimy turkey from the sandwich to eat, leaving the bread in the cardboard container that looked like French fries should come in it. Then in a few hours, I'd eat the white bread out of boredom.

The only mood boost I had was when I was walking back to my bed and accidentally looked over to the front desk. A CC was standing there in his stiff light blue dress shirt that was so overly starched it would keep its square shape on or off the hanger. His dark blue dress pants were tight, uncomfortably so, as if he wanted to replace them for a looser pair but his wife said his butt looked good in them, so he kept them to keep all the young recruits peeking.

I mistakenly made eye contact and he scream-whispered with gritted teeth, "What do you think you're looking at *blondie*?"

That was all that I needed to hear to be in a better mood. This guy—in his protein shake mustache cockiness—thought that he was God's greatest gift to earth and that his physical presence and rude attention was why I smiled as I continued back to my bed, but his overly pumped physique and arrogance that stemmed from some sort of insecurity had nothing to do with my inner joy. I was truly just happy to know that after five weeks, my blonde highlights were still intact.

And so went boot camp. It ended and all the tall people got leadership awards, as usual. Not that I was deserving of an award. I thrived at caring enough to get through it, was intrigued by its Stanford Prison Experiment-like atmosphere and enjoyed the physical exercise when nothing was right.

It was stressful, but fine. I went eight weeks without a cell phone, which would probably be a good disconnecting experience for any college graduate. I am sad to report that despite the Coast Guard label, not only did we never swim in the ocean during boot camp, but there were zero super fit Ashton Kutcher-like men hanging out in their own cheap and thin swim shorts. Was it all really worth it?

Boot camp had its purpose though, which in its essence is to get large numbers of people, from all types of backgrounds, through a program that takes away some of their individuality and provides a foundation for those who may have needed lessons in basic hygiene habits. With the boot camp experience, graduates are ready to go to the field, live closely among others, and focus on learning their job. I would soon learn that there were bigger obstacles than screaming CCs.

CHAPTER 3

GARY

New York City residents with homes in the Hamptons were notorious for leaving their bank account receipts next to the ATMs so everyone could see their million-dollar balances. My receipt revealing the $5000 Coast Guard signing bonus was probably incomprehensible to most of them. "Where are the rest of the zeros?"

ONE OF THE MOST valiant ocean rescues I was a part of involved a man named Gary, who radioed the unit in a panic that he was lost at sea. It was a summer night, which meant the Atlantic waters were calm and the wind was warm. The sun was about to set, and a golden hue filled the harbor.

"Mayday, mayday!" Gary interrupted as we tried to gather his information over the radio.

"What's your position, sir?" the watch stander asked again.

"Mayday Mayday. I'm at forty-one point zero six degrees north, seventy-one point ninety-one degrees west. Mayday, mayday!"

"Sir, we're going to have to ask you to stop saying Mayday over the public radio channel. That is an international distress signal. We understand you're distressed, and we are going to help you. Now, are there any medical emergencies on board?"

We continued to get his information, including a description of his vessel, which was essentially an eight-foot canoe that somehow had a radio on board.

The watch room where the radios were located was small. It had a two-person desk with windows that looked out at the harbor entrance. There was an oversized chart (map) table from the 1960s in the corner of the room with the local Montauk chart on top. The map was torn, marked, and needed replacing. The quicker watch standers used GoogleEarth at their desk to plot points and see where this large string of numbers landed the boat of interest. The old school Coasties wrestled with the ill-fitted chart table drawers to pull out the pencil and ruler for "real" position plotting. Their original methods usually required other old school Coasties checking the others' work and correcting it for more precision.

While taking down Gary's information, there were many people in the communications room eager for something to do. One person mapped out his position on the chart table, another took the coordinates to Google Earth, and one more person ran out of the watch room to look out the window on the side of the building. All concluded in varying amounts of time that Gary was not so much lost at sea, but was floating around the back of Lake Montauk, a small lake connected to our harbor that was bordered by summer homes.

After some back and forth on the radio, Gary still did not understand where he was. The sun had now set, and he was becoming more flustered.

"Mayda—I mean, Gary to Coast Guard Station Montauk. It's getting real dark out here."

Being the bored and sometimes caring little unit that we were, a small crew prepped to board our twenty five-foot boat to rescue Gary. This involved a risk management poll of the crew members as to how safe they felt for this mission:

"Environment! Walsh, how do you feel about the time of day, atmospheric and oceanic conditions, and other geographical hazards?"

"One," I replied to the one to ten scale of risk we all provided for every factor, then took the average to determine how risky of a mission it would be.

"Alright that does it for environment. Complexity! Evans, what is your score for complexity of this operation?"

"Three."

"A three? Are you fucking kidding me? Last month you gave our heavy weather training exercise a three and now you're giving *this* a three?" The boat crew leader chastised Evans, then remembered that the instructions for getting the risk assessment score from team members stated not to influence other people's scores, especially not to harass people for giving higher scores than you would expect. "Okay, so a three from fucking Evans. *Walsh*! What's your complexity score, and for the love of God don't say anything over one," he continued.

After we were in the green for our risk assessment, we stomped down the dock for the engineer to conduct engine checks. The rest of the boat crew untied the line from the dock and took off the buoy bumpers. The bumpers were shoved into their designated bins that were too small. Finally, we launched off in No Wake Zone speed, cruising over to Gary with a large spotlight and a loudspeaker.

"Gary," the crew announced through the megaphone as Gary waved both his arms in the air, "you are literally in three feet of water. We cannot get any closer. Are you able to step out of your canoe and drag it to shore?"

"I'm over here! Come this way!" Gary yelled, as if we couldn't see him under the giant spotlight that was surely blinding him.

"Unfortunately, we can't get any closer because our rudders will get stuck in the mud," the boat crew leader explained over the megaphone, in response to Gary's continued plea for closer assistance.

"Gary this is as far as we can go, would you like us to call the fire department to help you out of the water?"

After a little coaxing, Gary was able to walk his canoe to shore and the rescue concluded. Gary was safe and, miraculously, he was only a few doors down from his house, one of the ones that bordered Lake Montauk. The man who was lost at sea turned out to just need someone to shine a light to guide his way home. Much like the Coast Guard's history of manning America's lighthouses to guide home mariners desperate to reach shore, this little station continued the tradition by doing the same for Gary.

CHAPTER 4

WHAT AM I DOING HERE?

*After being stationed in the Hamptons and Key West, the only
people allowed to thank me for my service are
Alec Baldwin and Señor Frog.*

LIKE MANY WHO ARE not from New York, I was not familiar with
Long Island. *Montauk, Long Island?* I read in the welcome letter we
received from our units at the end of bootcamp. *Is that part of Staten
Island? Why are they claiming there is surf? Typical East Coast surf
culture, claiming they have awesome waves when most of the time the
waves are just better than nothing.*

A few weeks later, I arrived at an earthy, isolated surf and fishing
town, 100 miles from New York City, with more secrets than an
Agatha Christie murder mystery. Except for the summertime influx
of a few Jersey Shore-style partiers, it was nothing like Staten Island.
Long Island jetted out East from mainland New York for one hundred
miles, like an arm reaching out toward England. The giant peninsula,
connected to New York City by train, forms a north and south
side of the island. The north side was a long sound that connected
Connecticut with New York. The south side of the island was ideally
located for catching real ground swells rolling north from the open

water Atlantic Ocean. The waves arrived in monstrous sets instead of typical East Coast hurricane wave chaos. Montauk Point was at the very end of the island and the New York-famous Ditch Plains break took in the waves with a nice point break. I was pleasantly surprised.

Coast Guard Station Montauk was a small unit of around twenty-five people, and it operated more like a fire station than a military unit. The station was manned around the clock with a boat crew that was supposed to be either training or waiting and ready to respond to a distress call from mariners. The seafarers in this region could have been anywhere on the spectrum between hardened fishermen ready to go out in all conditions and Hamptons wives drinking wine out on their yachts for the afternoon while their husbands pleased their mistresses. Visually, the unit was one of those classic Coast Guard stations where every room had some version of wooden oars in various layouts as decorations. The grounds consisted of three small two-story buildings with off-white, wooden exteriors and rust-colored shingles, giving them a cottage-like feel. One building held the on-duty berthing, watch room, and command offices, another had the kitchen and off duty barracks, and the third was a poorly organized garage with a makeshift office building as a second floor like a mother-in-law suit you would add on if you did not want your mother-in-law to have air conditioning. I arrived in August just as one of the hurricanes that rocks the eastern end of the island each year was hitting. It was gray, extremely windy, and the parking lot was flooded upon my arrival.

In the exact hour that I walked into the unit, the chief of base was out on a training exercise that he mismanaged and would cause him to soon be relieved (fired). Little did he know that his big-wave exercises of riding through ten-foot seas in the forty-seven-foot aluminum tank-like boat was captured by a surf magazine photographer. The photos published by the surf magazine exposed that he had people onboard the Coast Guard boat who were not wearing proper safety gear. It wasn't long before the pictures made it to the desk of higher-level Coast Guard leadership and the careless commanding officer met his fate of early retirement.

Following that event, the unit was mostly in disarray. There were various temporary replacement leaders who were unable to understand the unit enough to make any progress against its misfit culture. I slowly learned that the unit was always and nearly forever in this state of disarray. It was a small group of eighteen-to-forty-year-olds living in a town of 3,000 that swelled to 300,000 in the summer party months. The unit had weak ties to any sort of broader organizational leadership within the Coast Guard. It was neglected in the worst way, causing it to go rogue. Sexism, racism, harassment, drug abuse, secrets, manipulation, and infidelity were daily occurrences, plus there were a few lethal bullies who, without proper leadership, could not be knocked off their pedestal and only gained traction with others impressed by their power. It was more than toxic; it was also alive and infectious. It seemed like I witnessed some outrageous behavior or statement every day . . .

"They need to stop letting women in the military. Definitely should not be on the boarding teams. You boys ready? Oh yeah, Walsh—uh, I forgot you were going out on this with us."

"They are both married, but she is sleeping with him so that she can keep her position here longer, you know, since her kids go to school in town. Everyone knows except their spouses. Just don't let on that you know, or she might start a rumor about you sleeping with him like she did with the last new girl. She even spread the rumor to the girl's new command! She thinks it throws people off her trail."

"He's selling oxy and some other stuff he gets from town, but only the other person who works in his office knows exactly what he's up to. She's buying painkillers and Adderall from him though so he's not worried."

"Bradley, they teach all the Negro kids in Jacksonville public schools to tie their shoelaces like that? You have got to be the dumbest motherfucker I've ever met. Don't smile, I'm not joking."

I don't know what I expected from my Coast Guard experience, but I began to question if I had really enlisted or if I had accidentally signed up to work at a shady bar next to a strip club in Akron. In college, there had been plenty of drug dealers and guys cheating on their girlfriends who were back at home, but this was different. I felt like I was on Jerry Springer, except I wasn't watching from the safety of my own home while the lies were exposed and the chairs flew on stage. I was having to involve myself with the people I had heard or seen were up to no good.

"Hey, SK1, I was told to come up here to get you to sign me in for this equipment," I said as I walked into the attic office above the garage. It was hot and stuffy, but the SKs (administrative personnel) seemed to like being separate from everyone else.

He looked at me and gave a slow smile with his slitted, bloodshot eyes; if he wasn't high on something, he was sure in a pleasant mood for being so tired. "Well, there you go, Walsh," he said in a slow drawl. "You let me know if you need anything, anything at all. I'm here to support the unit's needs."

He must be the one with the painkillers...

"Yeah! Let us know!" the other supply officer said. "Eager to help! You know how it is, so much to do, but we're here to work, you know! Get things done." She, in an opposite state of mind, went back to typing manically on the keyboard.

But what is she on?

My existence became an extreme yin and yang; one side was pure love for the region of Montauk and its character while the other was having an out-of-body, unreal experience dealing with the work environment. Any achievements the unit had were sadly knocked down by its controversies. In the first year, after the initial shock wore off, I did my own research on how to quit or how to get out. I even checked the consequences of going AWOL but having a dishonorable discharge did not seem like a status that would make it easy to find another job.

Do I have any disorders that would qualify me to get out? What would be the consequences if I faked a disorder so that I would be discharged? What would I even do if I left?

I hadn't applied to graduate school, and it was the fall, so even if I made it out, I'd have a whole year of no job, no apartment, no path. I had a bachelor's degree in psychology, which meant I could maybe find an entry level social work job, but since leaving California for the opposite side of the country in New York, I had practically no network to lean on. I did not want to go back to Ohio.

Well, my friend I graduated college with is working at Starbucks because she can't find a job . . . I guess this at least gives me a steady paycheck?

There was not going to be any quick fix. Or was there? About two years into my assignment, the Coast Guard announced a call where you could be honorably discharged, no questions asked. Apparently, they had overbooked the ranks, and with the budget cuts, were desperate to downsize.

Here is my out, I thought as I read the email addressed to the entire Coast Guard. It became the biggest talk among those at my level for the next few days, distracting each of us from the chaos of work life. *Was it worth it? Are you going to do it? Where will you go? You think I can get a job?* We had been complaining for so long and here was our opportunity to leave it all behind.

But it's been two years. I'm supposed to be at the training school I've been waiting for in less than a year, and so are you! We'll be out of this nightmare soon.

Only one woman at the unit took the early-out option. She was straight out of high school and had been secretly dating a much higher-ranking supervisor at a neighboring unit. He was about to transfer to another unit out of state. She was tired of the harassment people gave her about everything, from her bright red hair to her childish ways to her seeking safety in the arms of her creepy, much older boyfriend. He still hit on every new woman at the unit and didn't seem to mind the career risk he was taking by being with her. Knowing that she could live with him, she signed the papers and left. The rest of us stuck it out.

What was this world? Not only the military world, but the workforce after college, now with extreme restrictions and hierarchy. I was on my own during these years, or at least perceived it to be that way, not knowing that some from my boot camp class were experiencing the same lack of leadership and disillusion.

You, too, dealt with dudes not leaving you alone? Your supervisor was also selling drugs? We compared notes after Facebook reconnected us years later.

Somehow, there were still good memories. With the right limited crew for a training or a rescue, we could bask in a lack of nonsense while out on the ocean in the waves, away from the mayhem of the unit.

CHAPTER 5

LIABILITY

Veteran's Day brings on a lot of veteran's guilt for me because not only was I never in a war zone, but I was in the Coast Guard. Unfortunately, I have not helped improve the Coast Guard's reputation as a punchline for military jokes.

THE EVENING STARTED WHEN we got a distress call during the unit's favorite dinner of peanut chicken curry—our poor man's version of Thai food made with real Jif peanut butter. This meal had close to zero connection to the authentic cultural cuisine. I don't think the mess hall had curry spice jars and certainly Jif's half peanuts half hydrogenated oil ingredients were not what Thai restaurants were using to provide the hint of peanut in their peanut chicken curry dishes. Regardless, it was a popular dish.

With the call, we left our half-eaten dinners and rushed over to the communications room to get the details. The hardcore Coasties were excited to potentially have a real rescue. A fishing vessel was stalled forty nautical miles offshore (forty-six miles) and the large incoming swell meant they needed assistance before morning. It was clearly a dangerous situation because none of the fishing vessel's fellow fishing vessel friends agreed to go out to help them, which would have been protocol under normal weather conditions for the insular fishing communities of Montauk. The fishing communities usually preferred to avoid any type of law enforcement entity because many of them used cocaine instead of caffeine and some of them did not give a damn about fishing regulations.

It was April and the water was still cold, so a *mustang* suit was required. It was the military equivalent of a children's snow suit that you stepped into and pulled up to zip. It even included a cozy hood. With the right crew, we could jokingly sumo-style chest bump in these outfits and then whine like the kid in *A Christmas Story* that we couldn't put our arms down.

The four-person crew was supposed to be five, but we were short-staffed, and someone decided the smallest crew allowed would be fine.

The mechanic onboard was one of the unit's best and could handle any engine casualty as well as the deck work required for towing a large vessel. He was a perfectionist who was obsessed with being in good physical shape while also having a kindness and confidence that made him incredibly likeable. He was much like the ideal Coast Guard character Ashton Kutcher played in his movie *The Guardian*.

The other crew member, Smitty, was a bit of an *Arrested Development* character—he did not prioritize fitness, and tended to have beard stubble, which was not allowed by Coast Guard standards, whenever he thought no one would notice. He loved living in Montauk and getting a promotion meant he would have to transfer to a different unit. He decided it was in his best interest to remain an E-3—the lowest post-bootcamp rank in the Coast Guard—for eight years. Fortunately for the unit, in his lack of official career development, he honed his boat crew skills and was an asset to the unit with unprecedented area and historic knowledge, since most people leave the unit after four years.

The boat driver was usually respectable, but definitely a bit of a bro. A guy with a mix of high energy and early twenties laziness. He drank a lot of beers, he watched a lot of the New York Giants, and he fist-pumped occasionally like the nightclub-crawling characters of

Jersey Shore. He was your typical unpredictable youth, often completely unprofessional and inappropriate, but able to turn on the responsibility when required.

We mapped out where the stalled fishing vessel was—forty nautical miles offshore, right at our boat's operating limits. The team's risk-assessment process had a more serious tone than usual. It was growing dark outside, with a swell coming in, and we had limited information about what was wrong with the stalled vessel requesting assistance.

"All the scores added up, and we're in the high yellow, which means we're good to go," the boat driver said, excited to have an operation to lead, but slightly faking his confidence in himself. "Let's just call the chief to give him a heads up." He grabbed the 1990s corded phone and then walked out of the watch room, sliding shut the glass door on the cord and giving himself space so that no one could hear that he needed a pep talk from the chief.

After the call, bro boat driver slammed down the phone and jumped up in excitement to get our crew pumped for this voyage. We waddled down to the pier in our puffy mustang cold weather suits, our pockets bulging with extra gloves and wearing our ballcaps that did not fit proportionally with the rest of our bulky outfits. Just as we were taking off, the cook ran down the metal pier, his boots clanging as he shouted for us to wait a minute.

"You guys should take this stuff!" He handed us plastic grocery bags filled with apples, chips, and cans of Red Bull

"Where did you get the Red Bull?" one of the crew members asked.

"I ran out to 7-Eleven when I heard you got a serious radio call. Always prepared, am I right?" the chef said with a grin.

The cook was a put-together guy from New York City, who had way too much compassion to be a taken-for-granted cook in the Coast Guard. Although he was never the direct target of the racist remarks some of the others were prone to make, there's no doubt he overheard them and as a Black man, was deeply offended. Like the women at the unit, the rank system and lack of oversight made it nearly impossible for him to navigate making legitimate complaints, while also not facing backlash from the crew.

"Walsh, I can't believe these dudes," he'd say to me exasperated when I had kitchen cleaning duties. Then he'd go muttering and stirring whatever he was cooking in his large pots. When he was treated well, he cooked good food; when he was feeling used and abused, we got the basic meals of canned chili or hot dogs, served with an overly fake smile to take in all the complaints. This night, he was about to be off duty for the weekend, and he came to the crew's rescue with a few thoughtful snacks.

Handing the bags over the boat's railing as we started to drift away from the pier, the cook waved goodbye to us and watched our vessel leave the harbor. Four of us, ages nineteen to twenty-six, were setting off on quite a trip.

The sun was setting to the west as we headed east, as we glanced back, we watched the station's buildings become silhouettes on the edge of the harbor. All of us were glad to get a break from that place. Pretty soon it was dark, but we could still make out the shadows of land in the distance. Not much later, it was pitch black and there was no land in sight, even if we could have seen. Getting farther and farther from shore was peaceful until the waves started getting bigger below us. The boat driver became visibly more focused.

"Hey, I need you guys to pay attention. Bowdin, call things out when you see them on the radar. Walsh, keep an eye out up in front and let me know if you see any objects in the headlights," he said, demanding our vigilance.

We were two hours into the trip and still miles away from the distressed vessel. The waves crashed and we pushed ahead through them.

"Coast Guard vessel two-seven-nine, this is Station Montauk," we heard over the radio.

"Montauk, Vessel two-seven-nine, go ahead,"

"Yeah, two-seven-nine, we have a new position for the stalled vessel, let me know when you're ready."

The vessel in need of assistance had drifted to fifty nautical miles offshore—past the forty nautical mile limit of our boat. It was hard to have a conversation via radio while the boat was moving five feet up and then five feet down with the swells, but considering we were over halfway to the fishing vessel, it was decided to continue the operation.

We were all feeling good with the adrenaline and excitement. We had that bias of thinking it was easier to press on for twenty more miles than to return thirty miles, ignoring that once we pressed on twenty, we would be returning fifty with a fishing vessel in tow behind us. Hours later, we spotted the vessel, its dark green pilot house barely visible in the dark. It was fifty-plus feet of rusted fishing boat, rolling in the swells.

"Vessel Fishers Flight, this is Coast Guard two-seven-nine, where are your most secure forward cleats located?"

After receiving a garbled response on the radio, we circled their boat, pausing in the up and down motion of the sea to try to view their cleats in the darkness. Their crew was understandably listless, having been swayed by the ocean waves for a few hours and without power to at least maneuver to face the waves for a smoother ride.

In the black surroundings, the swells coming under our boat were unpredictable, throwing us in different directions. We sat, sizing up their boat and evaluating the best tactic for towing, while we were pitching up, down, and side to side, then slowly circling again. A decision was made about what to use for the tow as I looked aimlessly at this fishing vessel, imagining the scraggly men safe inside their pilot house while I was out up top our boat in the rain that had started to fall.

"Everyone understand the plan? *Walsh*!"

"Yes, all good, I'll have the watch up here," I said, hopeful I was repeating correctly what I had heard in the background of my thoughts.

It was time to prep the deck for towing. The Ashton Kutcher perfectionist extraordinaire and, Smitty, the Montauk-lifer went to the lower deck. I stayed with the bro boat driver in the open air above. I started to feel hot in my mustang, despite the cold air and drops of rain I welcomed to cool my flushed face. A feeling of discomfort grew inside, and I felt like I was starting to lose control. I breathed more deeply, trying to keep myself focused, watching for anything to go awry, but my inner organs grew hotter and the burning moved upward. I turned away from the radar screen, grabbed the railing, and in one heave, spewed a waterfall of curried chicken peanut vomit off the top deck and onto the lower. The precipitating brown liquid and chunks of our favorite dinner landed on the towing equipment below.

It was all gone from my body in one upchuck, but I remained fairly delirious.

"Aw, Walsh!" the boat driver said, correctly calculating I was not going to be helpful anymore.

One down out of four, but we still had the stellar crew of Ashton Kutcher and Smitty ready to mount a towing assault on the fishing vessel. Except, in a few short moments, we didn't have *any* crew anymore. In vision blurred by tears from the violent vomit and rain I could no longer wipe from my eyes because I had barf residue on my sleeves, I looked down to the lower deck and saw Ashton Kutcher, our all-star, heaving over the railing and spewing peanut chicken curry over the side into the ocean.

"Oh shit," the boat driver said. "That dude has the weakest stomach. That's not going to stop."

My vomit made Ashton Kutcher vomit for what felt like an hour. As he heaved up the peanut dish from dinner and the turkey chili from lunch, he tried to compose himself to pick up the tow line, but it was covered in my vomit, which made him vomit again. We were down to the bro boat driver and Smitty as we rocked back and forth and up and down, praying Smitty could get the towline over to the fishing vessel quickly and hoping the fishermen we were supposed to be rescuing did not notice that we were struggling.

With the darkness, waves, and weather, getting the tow line over to the other boat took more than one try. The boat driver was trying to keep his young-professional composure, yelling a mix of encouragement and threats

"Smitty!" he yelled, "You are doing great, but I am going to come down and punch you in the face if you don't get the line over on the next try!"

"*Smith*! You piece of shit! Get that goddamn line over! You've been doing this for how many fucking years? Come on! Your mom could get that line over with her eyes closed, you motherfucker!"

"*Smith! How do you fuck your wife without a dick? Come on, Buddy! I need you to get that tow line to the other boat!*"

Eventually, the line went over. The fishermen stumbled on the deck of their boat to hook it up on their cleats. It was getting close to midnight, and we were ready to return from now more than fifty nautical miles offshore. We started the trek back, and the boat driver forced himself to be a fully functioning and focused adult. The Ashton Kutcher with a sensitive stomach and I were inside the cabin, both rehydrating, but me more carefully because I wouldn't be able to pee off the side of the boat if it came down to needing to pee during our long trip back. Smith stayed up top to stand watch on the towline. With exactly one functioning crew member, the boat driver rightfully yelled obscenities from time to time as he navigated up top, embracing the elements, pulling a large fishing vessel behind him at night, in six-foot waves, with twenty feet of rope connecting our boat and the other vessel.

The towing evolution was a Coast Guard-approved version of a child tying one end of a rope to the seat of his bike and the other end to a skateboard for his friend to ride on as he rode the bike up and down hills. One poor choice in positioning by the boat driver or the wrong incoming wave would mean we'd have a fishing vessel rear ending us and we'd all be fucked.

I was too lightheaded to know what was happening. I only felt the slow speed we were moving and hoped the waves would ease.

They did eventually let up as the hours passed and the pitch-black night morphed into dawn. I woke up in the cabin, with smoother waves under us and the sun coming up. I was unknowingly cozied up to Ashton Kutcher. We had been sleeping next to each other in the standing position, each leaning into the other's comforter-like cold weather outfit. It would have been my secret dream come true if our mustang suits weren't soggily stuck together from stomach acid and partially digested food.

After opening my crusty eyes and rubbing away the gunk that I could with the backs of my unwashed hands, I left Ashton Kutcher to continue his upward slumber with the sun jetting in through the salt water splattered windows. Closing the cabin door behind me, it took all my effort to climb up the metal ladder to the top deck where there was a nausea-reducing morning breeze.

The bro boat driver was manically happy in his Oakley sunglasses and with three smashed cans of Red Bull on the floor below his high barstool-like seat behind the wheel. The caffeine must have been what mentally pushed him past his initial emotions of hating everyone on board for giving him more responsibility than he ever had before.

"What time is it?" I asked.

"Walsh, you owe me about fourteen hours of work. It's seven and we're almost home. By almost home, I mean we are going five miles an hour for another two hours, so now that you're up, you can take the tow watch."

It was only fair. Smitty with his beard scruff and now-baggy eyes had also been cracking Red Bulls for his overnight role of staring at the tow line connections and yelling changes to the boat driver in how the towed fishing vessel was riding so the boat driver could adjust course and speed.

"Coast Guard two-seven-nine, Station Montauk. We've got another boat coming out to meet you and take over the tow," we heard over the radio.

"Thank *God!*" our bro-boat driver said to no one in particular, looking up to the sky with his arms out, welcoming the relief. He was at his responsibility limits and the caffeine was losing its effects.

Upon their arrival, it took a few stumbling movements to remove the tow rope and hand it off. The four of us were finally free to ride back at a normal speed with innocent two-foot waves. It felt impossible that the ocean had been so tormenting hours prior.

Every operation called for a debrief. I learned from this op that no matter how you're feeling at the end, if you are the person who spewed peanut chicken curry over the wrong railing and this action caused others to spew their peanut chicken curry over the railing and down the side of the boat, the mission is not fully complete until *you* have cleaned the vomited peanut chicken curry off all boat surfaces.

The second lesson is more serious: to respect experience over status. With a little encouragement from the boat driver, Smitty, with his career lifetime at the unit with the lowest rank possible, saved all of our asses by watching that tow line all night.

The third and final lesson is that *if* you have a tight crew, led by an aspiring leader, who in his own development comes through more often than not, then despite your status as a complete liability through 90 percent of the operation, your shipmates will be waiting for you to finish cleaning before they sign off and go home. Their willingness to linger until the job is done will make you feel better than any Dramamine pill, which probably would not have prevented the ordeal anyway.

CHAPTER 6

THE DARKER DAYS

Why choose the Coast Guard? I was twenty-two, blonde, and fit. In most military services, that means guaranteed sexual harassment. Why not choose the one with the ocean breeze?

THE OCEAN BREEZE WAS nice. While looking for non-drug or alcohol-related opportunities to escape the life I was locked into for four years, I trained for a marathon. I didn't know I was training for a marathon, but eventually I found a marathon to sign up for so no one would comment that I was excessively exercising out my stress.

"Walsh, you run too much, you gotta hit the weights," as if hitting the weights didn't mean working out with five dudes in a fifteen-by-ten-foot room with limited ventilation.

Most people at the unit seemed to have hobbies of extramarital affairs or drug dealing that they were trying to hide. Their paranoia rarely manifested in a positive way. For me, running was the only thing that would get me off base while on a two- to three-day duty rotation. I would run for an hour in the morning to numb the annoyances that were sure to come. Then, I would run for two to three hours in the evening until the sun went down.

In the evenings, I tried to return exhausted to my dorm-like room to go to sleep, but unfortunately, my room was above the men's floor. Before I could reach my destination, I had to climb up the cheap plastic steps that held a permanent dusting of trimmed beard hair. The odor of sweat, shit, and Axe body wash strengthened with each step. There was no way to sneak past the guys on the floor because I was required to yell "Female!" before I reached their landing. This warned the guys to put on pants and ensured I could not get upstairs without some form of degrading comment.

"*Walsh*! What the heck were you doing just now, sneaking off to get some action at the gas station? There's no way you ran that whole time. I'm gonna catch you fucking off and you're gonna get it; two a.m. shifts the rest of your time here. I'm not fucking joking."

"*Walsh*! We heard the floor creaking last night. Was Hart (the other female who sometimes shared the space) going down on you? You girls up there getting down in each other's pussies? I know you were; I can hear it sometimes."

"*Walsh*! You never hang out with us down here. What, you're too good for us? Running the East Hampton Marathon? I hope you cramp up and can't finish the race and watch all the rest of the runners pass you."

It was probably a good thing the search and rescue opportunities were slow at that unit because I am not sure I would have had the energy to take part in daily responses. Running numbed me enough to tolerate the environment and tiredly laugh off the commentary until I could get off duty and go surf.

There were many problems at this unit—from sexual harassment and racism to ego-tripping idiots. Many were out in the open, like racist remarks in the mess hall and sexual innuendo that caused the decent people to look down at the floor. Other fucked-up things were just kind of fucked up. During one of my exams, I was quizzed in-person by a three-person board who asked questions to confirm my knowledge of the exam topic.

"Walsh, what are the dimensions of the *fffrrrttt*," one examiner decided to rip a huge fart in the middle of asking me a question.

It wasn't the kind of accidental bonding fart where everyone laughs and snickers afterwards; it was an aggressive fart. This fart was intentional and meant to signal that I didn't matter; loud and clear that I was not going to receive any respect. All of these incidents were the symptoms of the deeper toxicity weaving throughout the unit—a snake slithering and wrapping its prey.

"Walsh! What happened in there?" A halfway decent member who was on the exam training board came up to me a day later.

"Um, I did the best I could," I replied.

"You barely nailed the required number of questions," he said.

"I really don't care."

"What's wrong? You know all that stuff, why didn't you take it seriously?" he said, having witnessed the disrespect throughout the exam and ignoring it.

"You want *me* to take it seriously! Okay, BM2, I will take it seriously when people aren't ripping ass in the middle of my questions," I responded. He was cool enough to vent to, but not cool enough that I could end it with a casual "fuck off."

They thrived on power and directing their subordinates just because they could, like a mean girl playing house and demanding she was the mom and all the kids had to listen.

Yet, like many issues in the military, the sexual harassment side of power trips was ignored by political leaders and was not of interest to the general population. Each year since 9/11, most civilians become more and more disconnected from our armed services.

The sexual assault issue and its depth was documented and presented in the 2012 film *The Invisible War*, a story of the rape epidemic in the military. Some military services showed the film it in their annual sexual harassment training course, the way an adult gives a child a book about sex instead of having an uncomfortable conversation to provide a full understanding of the topic.

Outside the military, the film raised approximately zero eyebrows, bringing in barely over $70,000 at the box office. Casual sexual harassment and assault was like the drug abuse problem in the United States; it would only receive attention once upper-class White people were suffering from it. Unless it's wealthy, White celebrities who are being sexually assaulted, it has no place in the news. Military women must not have had the right hashtag. #UsToo.

As an enlisted college graduate, I experienced a weird combination of knowing the unit was going in the wrong direction but having no real-world experience to know what to do about it. One of the assaulters in Station Montauk, BM2 Twinley, would isolate the few women at the unit from each other with rumors that another woman was talking shit or acting against the other's best interest. Interactions like this were common:

"Yeah, Walsh said that I should give you the night shifts because you're younger."

"What a bitch, that's not fair, you should give her the night shifts because she's always getting away with everything."

Then I'd come in and try to greet her. "Hey! How was the weekend?"

"You told them I should get the night shifts? Come on, that's not fair."

"I didn't say . . ."

"*Ladies*! Quit your cat fighting," a guy from below would yell, "get down here and do your part in cleaning up so I can go home."

Most of the men at the unit could talk *during a meeting* for thirty minutes about their weekend fishing trips, arguing about the best bait, but when it came to the women having a conversation about issues, we were interrupted as being unproductive.

I felt responsible for the rifts this type of interference caused because I could see what was happening and yet had no communications channels available to reach respectable people at higher levels for guidance, no trusted mentor to run things by, and no gauge of how bad things were at the unit beyond what I was experiencing. I guess I could have measured it by the number of pounds I lost running away stress.

I was on watch one afternoon and sitting at the computer when the crew came in to do their risk assessment for a training session. When everyone looked away at the map that they were going over, BM2 Twinley put his hand on my shoulder near my neck. His grip was firm, and his fingers dug in, not exactly a pat on the back kind of touch. I stiffened my body and slowly rolled my chair to the side so he would have to move his hand off.

One Sunday morning I walked into the main seaside cottage-like building on base and heard BM2 Twinley call out to me from an office. Sundays were usually low key because the command was off work for the weekend.

"Walsh, why don't ya step into my office?"

I walked down the hall and into the office, just past the door frame. It wasn't his office; it was a leadership office he took over when no one was around. My hair was wet and salty. I was in sweats, about to go shower and get ready. I had asked to go surfing for my morning workout since the rest of the crew was going to take the afternoon off to watch football.

"You gonna thank me for letting you go do that?" he said.

"Oh yeah! Of course, thanks, surfing is always a good way to start the day. I'll be dressed out and ready to stand watch in ten minutes" I said, still high from a short session of cold New York waves.

"You're not going to thank me another way?" he asked, pushing himself back from the desk and gesturing toward his crotch. He gave a creepy smile that started to turn angry as seconds passed and I did not respond. He put his hands down on the arms of the chair and began to push himself up towards me.

What is happening?

I froze. I could not take a breath; I could not even blink. My mouth was open to delay my response with an "uh," but I could not make a sound. My mind stalled as if I had pressed pause. It was just me and him in the building. It felt like the house in the 1980s *Beetle Juice* movie: isolated, up on stilts surrounded by a desert full of dangerous creatures.

Uh. What. What the fuck do I say? What do I do?

I couldn't think of the first step to get out of this. I needed my body to leave the room, then leave the building, then leave the base, then leave Long Island, the leave this life. His face got angrier as he left his chair and began to move toward me. I didn't think I'd win a fight against him. Unless I immediately kicked him in the balls and maybe elbowed him in the face really hard. But damn, that would lead to an investigation into my aggression, which would probably inhibit me from ever getting out of this place. I felt a cool breeze from behind.

"*Giants!*"

"*Jets! Jets! Jets!*"

The back door to the outside had swung open and these idiots came back from breakfast, yelling about their New York football rivalries, just in time. Their interruption jolted me back in control of myself. I slid out of the room and followed those morons upstairs, drafting on their group so that BM2 couldn't approach me. I could not put it all together in the moment. I had thought he was just in his power-granting mood and that's why surfing was given the okay. Any sort of sexual favor reciprocity was not what I had intended whatsoever.

Am I naive? Am I that dumb to think he just wanted to do something reasonable? I am such an idiot.

I feel like I let myself be manipulated out of fear of the military hierarchy and fear of causing more problems that would have kept me at the unit longer. Fear that if I brought things up, I'd have to move to a new unit and leave the nearby surfing that at least gave me some friends and sanity. I was not certain that I had enough of the inappropriate activity documented to prove that this person clearly crossed a line. I did not see how reporting it would do anything but cause more problems, more anxiety, and more stress. All of these thoughts were confirmed when I ran it by the guy I was dating, who was also in the Coast Guard.

"He keeps giving me the overnight shifts when I don't answer his texts. What am I supposed to do?"

"What do they say?"

"One says, 'Walsh, you need to sign the form you submitted before I can process it.' Then the next talks about how good my ass looked when I walked into the unit in my UGG boots. He wasn't even in his office yet. He must have been watching from his car while I was walking in. He's such a creep."

"That's just how he is. You'll be out of here soon. Just let it go," he replied.

"Alright. I will *just* let him keep being intimidating and gross. You know his wife is pregnant?"

I let it go.

"Ms. Walsh, this is Coast Guard Investigative Services, please give us a call back at your earliest convenience." The voice mail made my chest tighten.

What did I do? What could I have possibly done? All I've been doing is working. Well, I did go out drinking a few times. Oh shit, and I hooked up with that pilot . . .

It was two years after leaving Montauk. I had finished intelligence school and was wrapping up my tour in Key West, Florida, ready to leave the Coast Guard and move on from the uniform.

What is this about?

The voicemail was like an ex-boyfriend calling on a lonely night: you think it's over, you move on, then you get dragged back in. The investigator had a list of around fifteen women BM2 Twinley had assaulted throughout his career and asked if I had also been affected. I called them back.

"But what happened? How did this come up?" I asked.

"He assaulted Ms. Brooks at Station Montauk.

"Assaulted?"

"He attacked her."

Brooks was the woman who reported to the unit right before I left. She was my replacement when I left for intelligence school. She was like me, a college graduate who joined, completed boot camp, arrived in Montauk, and started to question her decision to join in the first place.

"You still dress like a college student!" she teased me one day as I got off duty and left for the gym.

"I'm only twenty-five!" I shot back, refreshed by her playful grin and good-natured humor.

In the time we overlapped at the unit, I trained her on what it means when you have kitchen duty and started introducing her to what I knew about being on the boat crew. I failed to train her against predators and provide guidance on how not to get raped. My prior silence on this man's inappropriate behavior left him on the prowl for other prey.

With the evidence the investigator gathered, the attacker went to a court martial (trial). He pled and was found guilty of Article 93 (Cruelty and Maltreatment), Article 120 (Rape and Sexual Assault—as a lesser included offense), and Article 128 (Assault). He was demoted to the lowest rank, spent ten months in confinement, and was discharged with bad conduct.

CHAPTER 7

WANT FRIES WITH THOSE LEADERSHIP SKILLS?

I need more people to be on antidepressants because everyone is up and excited about Sunday brunch while I'm over here thinking about how I'm deployed, no one is going to be there when I get back, and a person who is clinically mentally unstable is in charge of my life.

ON THE BETTER DAYS, being at a small boat station was like being on a version of *The Office*, if that TV show had involved a hierarchy of disgruntled janitors who were constantly cleaning things that were already clean because there was no actual work to do.

We had a schedule in which one crew would work a few days, then the other would take over. These takeovers focused on checking whether the first crew left everything clean and ready for the next crew, from the stairs in the barracks to the windows on the boat. It seemed like a good idea to do this to maintain order—until you added in twenty-two-year-old, testosterone-filled, power-seeking males with no supervision looking to assert their dominance and maintain their spot at the top of the food chain by hassling anyone who, by rank, they were allowed to hassle. Even the high-testosterone women got in on the cleanliness ego battles. Lucky for a few of us, most of the time, these guys and one gal were dense as rocks.

Simple Green was the cleaning product of choice for our station. It was sold by the barrel and supposed to be heavily watered down before use. Naturally, people at this unit took shortcuts whenever possible, so the Simple Green bottles available were overly concentrated. The high concentration resulted in fumes that were as toxic as a nontoxic product could be. Hours later, the scent still hung in the air and stayed lined in your nose.

One morning, my colleague, Harley, and I grabbed our trusty green spray bottles and cleaned the inside of the small boat in preparation for the crew turnover. We made sure it was spotless so we could be relieved and get home on time. Harley was a good kid from Boston who, based on his chill pace of speaking and tendency to get the giggles when something was ridiculous, probably smoked a bit of weed growing up. Even with his pace, he was sharp, plus had common sense and decency.

The first day Harley was at the unit, he commented in his Boston accent about how the command was completely messed up.

"Walsh, what the fuck is this place? I went to three different offices, each person told me what I needed was in the other office. Their offices are literally in the same hallway and no one is doing shit. Does the training officer always have his bare feet up on the desk? That's disgusting. Why does his room wreak of body odor and peanut butter? And why are Storekeeper's eyes glassy as fuck?"

I knew from his rant that I could trust him.

One early morning, we were on the boat cleaning, "Walsh, this *has* to be the cleanest boat in the fleet! Say a prayer that we can go home already," Harley said as he gave the windows a few last circular polishes to clear the streaks from the window cleaner. "I had that two a.m. round every night the last few days. I'm running on fumes and Redbull, but *damn,* look at this masterpiece," Harley did a Vanna White imitation, showing me the dashboard that hadn't been that clean probably since it arrived at the unit.

The morning was tranquil and windless. The water was still, except for the rusty fishing vessels slowly returning to their respective docks after their overnight expeditions. The biggest wake that morning would be caused by the oncoming supervisor, who was the person designated to approve our cleaning. Her tendencies included compensating for something in her life by being fiercely hierarchical, like we were children playing dress-up and she was the mean and abusive mom who took it too far. This woman was usually too busy obnoxiously regulating everyone on meaningless things to notice the irony that she was completely out of the Coast Guard's weight regulations while holding everyone else to her imaginary standards.

As she stepped on to begin her inspection, the small twenty-five-foot boat, with its aluminum structure and orange bumper, swayed from the change in buoyancy. Most people had to crouch inside the structure, but her short and stout figure stood stiff with her chest puffed out, and she moved her eyes in a visual inspection. Unsurprisingly, our cleaning was not to her high standards of care. She then ran her finger along the window edge, picked up zero salt, dust, or debris and proceeded to blow nonexistent particles off her finger.

"It's not good enough. You better clean it good or I'm going to hold you here until lunchtime. I can do that, you know. They said I'm in charge of approving all the cleaning today and maybe next shift too. They might make me the permanent person to approve all the unit cleaning. I don't *care* if any of you were up all night on watch, *no one* gets to go home until *I* say it is all good," she said, oozing with childish ruthlessness.

My colleague and I rolled our eyes, which had become our most common facial expression. She stomped back up the dock, giving us time to keep cleaning. We sat in the seats on this inside of the boat looked out at the harbor. The sun had fully risen, and we ached to go home to rest. After fifteen minutes of watching the boats come in and out of the harbor, the soft up and down of the water below us soothing our irritation, we picked up our Simple Green bottles. Harley and I sprayed the air like a cloud of perfume you walk through before a big date, then moved to the front of the cabin to let the mist settle.

"There's no way this shit is nontoxic," Harley coughed, "oh god, too much," he waved his hands to disperse the cloud.

The big bad BM3 (boatswains mate third class, the lowest petty officer rank) came back, trudging down the dock with her hands on her hips in a power pose. No doubt she'd been harassed by her own peers for her weight and not being good at her job. In some people, receiving that type of harassment builds a sense of empathy for others, but for her, it seemed to have been a lesson in how she should treat other people. When she first arrived at the unit, I tried being pleasant to see if it would get her off my back:

"BM3, how's your morning?" I asked one day as I was leaving shift and she was in the communications room Googling *ephedrine dietary supplement and Coast Guard policy.*

"You're supposed to be down at the boats working. I'm a BM3, that means I don't have to do that work that *you're* supposed to be doing. So why don't you get down there and do it already," she stood up in her famous power pose, leaned toward me, and failed to notice that I had all my bags and was leaving.

"Totally. I'm actually on the off-going shift, I'll see you in a few days!"

For the long term, avoidance and letting her perceive submission were the easiest coping mechanisms. It was all so exhausting. After failing at kindness, the only way I could humanize her was to consider a psychological diagnoses that fit her behavior. Psychosis was a mental issue that caused you to lose touch with reality. Early signs were suspiciousness or unease around others as well as a lack of self-care or hygiene. Could it be? Even with my unofficial diagnosis, I couldn't muster much empathy and accepted that there are just some people in the world who are bad off and will continue to be that way. I had disliked people before in my life, but intense resentment was new, yet seemed fair for where I was in life.

Shuffling sideways through the door, she ran her finger along the other windowsill, inspecting it like a morbid Mary Poppins. After a long pause for drama's sake, she told us it was good, and we were free to go. "Don't even *try* to do a light cleaning job on *me* next time," she scolded. Harley and I held in our eye rolls; we were too tired to cause any problems. The Simple Green scent was enough to please this woman. I imagined she was disappointed there wasn't any real salt residue left on the windows for her to scrape and sprinkle on her post-inspection snack of last night's french fries.

CHAPTER 8

MONTAUK WINTERS

My parents have been mostly okay with my life decisions. I think their main worry was I'd decide to end my life early. Not only am I still here, but I can pay my rent. The bar is low.

MONTAUK, NEW YORK WAS deathly cold in the winter. The wind gusts came from every direction and were strong enough to break your spirit while you were outside, then loud enough to still haunt you while you were inside. It was fucking cold. I read that the Native Americans on Long Island *avoided* Montauk in the winter. Instead, they posted up further west near what is now the East Hampton Starbucks to wait it out until the spring thaw calmed the icy and erratic hurricane-force winds. I followed in their tracks in the winters, hunkering down at the East Hampton Starbucks for hours at a time on my days off.

Despite the cold and the fact that nearly all civilian boats in the area were iced in until March, our unit continued to train year-round. I understood the need to be ready, however, I wasn't all about it. We had a forty-seven-foot motor lifeboat and to stay qualified as a crew member, we had to rack up hours on the boat, acting out various scenarios, such as retrieving someone from the water and towing a boat that had broken down. It was all very pleasant and lovely in the summer, cruising through the waves, with the salt water refreshingly splashing on your face. In the winter, however, going out on the boat might as well have been an expedition to the arctic with obstacles in the style of the *Legends of the Hidden Temple* game show. If you survived the iced-over dock, you were sure to slip on the exposed metal deck of the boat that could not be repaired with grip tape until spring.

One particularly frosty outing occurred when we didn't need training hours, but someone insisted we did. The insister was of junior rank who enjoyed exerting his authority over others of even more junior rank. He took pride in casually disregarding safety and practicality for the sake of his interpretation of leadership. No other boats were out on the water these days, and if anyone was going to need saving from the ocean, it was going to be us. Despite this, five of us gathered in the communications room to run through the risks of the training and score them, then add the highest to see where we landed on the risk scale. We were high, of course, but, of course, went out anyway.

"*Walsh*! Safety. Give me a number."

"Six."

"*Six*? A fucking six? What are we in *The Perfect Storm* right now? We got eight-foot waves rolling in? It's seriously two-foot waves, plus, I just finished heavy weather training school. I'm fresh."

"The water temp is thirty-eight degrees, air temp hasn't broken twenty, and we can't wear gloves when working the tow line," I shrugged. I withheld commenting on how just finishing school didn't exactly count as the equivalent of having years of real-world experience.

We put on our rubber-neckline dry suits that were red with black knee patches. They had a bit of an astronaut suit look to them. Unlike the cushy and warm mustang suits that fit over your uniform like a snowsuit, the drysuit was tight and the rubber neck felt like it had a suction on you. If it did not suffocate me pulling it down and on, it almost always pulled out a chunk of my hair while using all my arm strength trying to pull it up and over my face to get it off.

Down at the dock, we silently chipped away at the ice-covered rope that held the boat to the pier. It was too cold to complain and objecting would only fuel the boat driver in charge's desire to push through on this trip. The water in the harbor was not frozen, but it was looking frosty, like one more degree lower and it would be a giant slushee. We got out of the harbor. The air was a blend of snow, ice, and wind. The boat had a cabin from where you could drive inside and avoid the elements, however the same thoughtful leader who insisted on doing this training naturally insisted we all navigate from outside.

My colleague, who was from sunny Miami, and I sat at the back of the boat looking at the icy wake we were creating, the two rudders churning up ice chunks like a blender. He regularly reminisced about the warm waters of Florida.

"If I fall in," he said, "just keep going."

With that, he summed up winter life at Station Montauk.

CHAPTER 9

SUMMER FREEDOM

The great thing about the Coast Guard is that once you get past the creeps and hard-core law enforcement members, it's mostly full of people who like turtles and the ocean.

BEING IN YOUR TWENTIES means neurologically not being able to think more than a few steps ahead. Being an entire unit of people mostly under the age of thirty, it was a dangerous and glorious existence whether on duty or off.

My reservist friend, Anna, would come into town one weekend a month and provide some sanity.

"Caroline! How are you?" she would greet me early in the mornings when I would come into the kitchen to say hi before breakfast officially started. She always started the weekend happy and fresh, even with her five o'clock wakeup that followed her eight-hour drive from Pennsylvania. Anna had a fun Shirley Temple spunk to her, with curly light brown hair and her natural-colored lipstick.

"I brought my bike! I'm so excited we can go explore tonight!" she exclaimed, her body contorted to talk to me while also tending to the four pans she had going on the stovetop.

Anna had been active duty and understood what was up with this unit. She went about her business ignoring rude comments, knowing she could leave to return to her saner world on Sunday night.

"Ugh, these eggs are burned, FS2. What, you come here on the weekend to slack off and earn your reserve pay?"

"What was that?" she would lean away from the stove pretending she hadn't been able to hear, hoping it wasn't worth repeating. She hardly made enough money on the weekends to pay for her drive to the unit.

"Never mind," one the guys would grumble, not yet caffeinated enough to cause trouble.

Anna and I became quick friends, talking about school and, overall, both of us were decent people. It was funny how it didn't take much to be excited to connect with anyone normal, especially a female who could relate.

Anna was smart, but like me, had no maritime background before joining the Coast Guard. On her first assignment on a ship, she was left to drive it after being told she should find something on the horizon toward which she could steer the boat. This would help keep this large ship with hundreds of people onboard going in the right direction during their six-month deployment. The object Anna chose was a cloud.

She and I discovered that we both had picked up an interest in road biking, so on one of her trips she brought her bike so we could go on an adventure after her workday was over. Her 5:00 a.m. start meant she was ready to check out at 5:00 p.m., leaving the crew with the option to order pizza since she wasn't getting any appreciation.

It was a late summer evening, warm air with a cool breeze and the sun was starting to set. We decided a bike ride from Montauk to Amagansett along the coastal road would be amazing.

The way to Amagansett *was* amazing through all twelve miles of country road; the sun's golden hour made the trees along the road a crisp green and watching the sun start to dip below the ocean was magical. We arrived and sat on a bench in the near dark and hydrated. She had to work at five o'clock the next morning, so we decided to forgo a drink and start the trek back.

We got about four miles in and it became too dark to see the road in front of us. We had planned our sunset bike ride without considering how we would get back once the sun had set. Being road bike amateurs, neither of us had a headlight; all we had was her red blinking light for the back of the bike. With that, she took the rear and I had the lead. It was then pitch black and the country road had no streetlights. Being built on top of sand, the blacktop road was cracked with potholes that we could not see. The only thing that saved us was the occasional passing car, whose headlights would help us see about twenty feet of the road ahead, while also undoing all the night vision we had just gained.

Neither of us spoke except to warn the other of dangers. It was the most intense mission of our Coast Guard careers. We had gone out and we really wanted to get back without going over the handlebars. I'm pretty sure we both had cell phones on us but calling one of the guys to pick us up didn't even cross our minds, which shows you how much we trusted the guys in that unit. There were not yet Lyfts or Ubers, so we were really screwed.

We somehow made it back unharmed. We didn't fully recognize how lucky we were until the next morning when I came in for coffee and be both discussed how that was dumb and we definitely could have died by pothole or by getting hit by a car.

Our fun-loving twenties mindset set us up to start the adventure, but didn't lead us to the safest return. It wasn't exactly guiding ourselves by a cloud, but it might as well have been.

CHAPTER 10

DON'T YOU KNOW THAT YOU'RE TOXIC?

I always regretted that I wasn't involved in more labs while I was an undergraduate student in psychology. Little did I know that signing my Coast Guard contract would put me in a social psychology lab-like setting for over four years.

REFLECTING ON HOW THIS unit functioned taught me how physical location does not make a place immune from the toxic environment in which they operate. Station Montauk, with its isolation and lack of mission for months at a time, was never going to be a place where many could thrive. It was located at the eastern end of everything in a place remote enough that during the 1918 Spanish Flu pandemic, the military sent soldiers there to quarantine. Without a huge shift in how this unit was run—perhaps like a unit in the Florida Keys that was only up and running during the tourist high seasons, when boredom would not be so quick to occur—we were always going to struggle.

"Be careful in the winters," warned the guy from the unit who had picked me up from the train station upon my initial arrival and was giving me a driving tour around Montauk, along with his advice.

"It's dangerous in the water? Or just really cold?" I asked.

"Not that; just don't get in trouble. Find something to keep you busy. Remember that." His eyes looked out the window as if he was regretting something, "and get your East Hampton parking pass; if you like to surf, you're going to need it."

Being at this unit also showed me the importance of communication and interaction with leadership.

"Who are we picking up from the Sector?" I asked. We were making the trek to our *boss* unit on the forty-seven-foot boat across the Long Island Sound.

"Captain something. I don't know any of those guys. Some officers are coming out to pretend they want to know how we are doing."

The lead unit for the area was across the Long Island Sound from us—an hour boat ride or a multi hour car trip. The officers opted for the boat ride so once we picked them up, we headed back to the unit via boat.

"Maybe Captain Upchuck should have taken the car trip," the boat driver commented. It was awkward, the wind had picked up and the swell was churning in the sound, making it a bumpy ride back to our station. Two of the three officers onboard were puking off the side of the boat as we continued on.

It might not have seemed important for leaders of the lead unit to visit this little place with more frequency, but maybe a little more interaction would have revealed some of the dysfunction that could have been fixed before formal measures had to be taken. A few additional exchanges between junior people at the two units could have provided an informal check as to whether what one person was experiencing was usual military life or should not have been accepted as the norm.

Being in the Coast Guard, I experienced a mix of both military and law enforcement cultures and, of course, the worst tends to stay with you. One time I was screamed at—spit-flying-in-my-face screaming—in front of the command hallway by a low-mid ranking member for nearly no reason.

"Walsh! You worthless piece of shit. Why would I want to help you out? This is the dumbest fucking thing I've ever had to do. You aren't worth anything. I'm not joking. I hope you fucking fail OCS!"

No one came out of their office to see what was happening, let alone correct his tantrum. This member was upset he had to get up early for a boat trip across the Long Island Sound. The purpose of the trip was to take me to a CG related medical appointment, hence I was the reason he had to get up early and his adult tantrum ensued. In a comical light, he was a Farva from *Super Troopers*, putting soap in the rookies' coffee. However, in the darker moments, he was a menace that leadership did not control and contributed to the deterioration of the morale and values of the entire unit. Those who wanted to feel powerful sided with him to avoid his wrath.

I was low ranking and a woman. Except for being White, I had nothing going for me in terms of military culture favorites. I thought I was supposed to at least have some *in-group* favoritism, social-psychology-speaking, considering I was part of the unit and was not a civilian. However, I was never let in. Clearly, I wasn't considered part of his team. Why else did my existence anger him? I was applying to Officer Candidate School (OCS). After the 2008 economic disaster there was an influx of people enlisting after college and people like this guy didn't know how to place us. Most of the college grads enlisted with a humbled attitude, very aware that our degree, which wasn't helping us get a job on the outside, wasn't an essential prerequisite to running rescue operations.

Not all who wander are lost. Except lieutenants, they are probably lost.

The normal teasing of officers (higher rank managerial roles) by enlisted was expected, but not intense anger, especially at a unit that was hardly affected by anyone at the officer level. I felt like I was the scapegoat for the problems that the US economic divide caused for him, a representation of the perceived elitism of an increasingly expensive college education. I couldn't help but wonder if this was personal or if this person viewed himself as falling behind because I was moving up.

Whoever was in charge did not regulate the outbursts. Maybe they did not care he was a problem? They chose to feign ignorance that he was a problem? They had too many other problems to deal with? They did not know how to use the system to control this person who was a problem? They didn't know where to begin and were hiding their own corruption?

Most of the first few years in the Coast Guard, I felt like I was in the Stanford Prison Experiment, an experiment when researchers put college students in roles as either guards or prisoners and ended up having to end the experiment early because the guards became too domineering in their roles. It was a unit full of people absorbing power and using it to fill the void derived from whatever inferiority complex they had.

"I think this unit needs a new start—like burn down the buildings, get rid of everyone, and start over completely," I proposed to a colleague.

"Agreed, but I'm not sure that idea is going to get much traction," he replied. "These are historic buildings, so someone might have a problem with the burning down part. Probably wouldn't fit in the budget anyway."

The only way I could see this toxic unit improving is if they rid it of everyone and start fresh with respectable people, high quality leadership, and an adjusted mission to suit the environment. If the buildings weren't so historic, a good demolition could have made for a less-segregated workspace. It might have also cleared the karma from someone who supposedly hanged themselves in the garage.

After about one year there, I had another stroke of national catastrophe luck. Something as dreadful and damaging as the Swine Flu, which provided me four days of peace in bootcamp, was about to give me a break from Montauk—the Deepwater Horizon oil spill. Sweet home Alabama, the white sand shores, now doused in oil, were calling.

CHAPTER 11

SWEET TEMPORARY HOME ALABAMA

The therapist diagnosed me with mild PTSD . . .
is that a Coast Guard-specific diagnosis?

THE DEEPWATER HORIZON OIL spill disaster, ironically, provided some normalcy for me at last. It was August 2010, four months after the disaster, but only *one* month after they had capped the leak. It wasn't fully sealed until September. During those eighty-seven days, 200 million gallons of crude oil were released into the ocean, making it the largest oil spill and environmental disaster in US history. Eleven people died and seventeen were injured because British Petroleum created a culture of profit over safety, according to federal investigators. BP was the villain while the Coast Guard led a unified command that included organizing and directing a fleet of over 6,000 vessels. Their lessons learned from the incident resulted in even better responses to future disasters. I was taken from the emotionally toxic corner of one of the Coast Guard's small response teams to a physically toxic environmental disaster that was one of the Coast Guard's most professional and well-led national stage responses.

You want me to sit in an office and work on a strategic project without daily harassment? You don't want me to clean. Anything? Are you sure? I'll wipe down the desks. I know, I don't have to do that. I'll just clean them at the end of the day. Oh, there are janitors who do that. I get it. I'll show up, do my work, and then leave without anyone having a power tripping mental breakdown at my expense. It might take some time for me to adjust to all this.

I arrived in Alabama with hesitant enthusiasm—eager to get away from my unit but hesitant that I could end up working with the same type of venomous people. After a few days of working on a good team, I lost my hesitancy and enthusiastically extended my orders multiple times to continue working on the response. Not only did the work feel important, but there was something in my workdays I couldn't identify. Respect? Compassion? Autonomy? It finally felt good to be at work.

The contractors I worked with were colorful locals of Mobile, Alabama. One woman, mildly heavy with spiky, dyed, dark auburn hair, who always wore floral blouses, loved a good controversy. One morning, in her polite Southern accent, she talked for ten minutes about how someone just told her she had been saying "Macaroni Grill" wrong. She was told it was actually spelled and pronounced the "Mar-coni Grill."

"Can you believe that? *MAR-coni.* All these people sayin' it wrong this whole time! Since it began, really!"

The next day in our documentation work, which consisted of going through various boxes of all kinds of papers and documents from recently closed offices, she gasped.

"Well, my oh my." It was a Macaroni Grill menu. She put her hand to her chest, "My lord, Jesus forgive me. I guess it is Mac-aroni after all," she shook her head. My Coast Guard colleagues and I were in awe and delight that the Macaroni Grill pronunciation could be the most dramatic event of the day.

I spent six months in the glorious Floribama (Florida + Alabama) region working on the documentation team. My project team and its leadership served as a lesson in what motivated employees. The comfort I had at work developed from mutual trust, autonomy, and a got-your-back mindset. All were incredibly intrinsically motivating. Making a little extra cash in per diem didn't *hurt* my motivation either, but it was not the driver. Also motivating was the threat of having to return to Station Montauk, a ridiculous work environment filled with harassment and manual labor. And, on top of that, each passing month brought me closer to returning to a frigid Montauk winter.

I can see the headline now: *How to Motivate Your Employees: Threaten that the Alternative is Chipping Ice off Docks in 10 Degree Weather with Twenty-Five knot Winds.* Threat as motivation might not be worthy of a Harvard Business Review article, but the fear of returning to Montauk was there and it made me loyal and productive.

The assignment started with a group of fifty Coast Guard personnel who flew in from all over the country and then traveled three hours to the city of Mobile, where we attended the morning meeting at the Mobile Incident Command Post. It was a professional briefing room with rows of seats and a large monitor cycling through the oil spill response updates.

"Good morning, welcome to the Incident Command Center, Mobile. I want to thank you all for traveling down here to respond. That's what a Coastie does! With the way the response has evolved, however, your service will no longer be needed. Our administrative personnel will be arranging each of you to return to your home unit tomorrow. *Semper Paratus.*"

I guess they were *Semper Paratus*, "always prepared," with fifty extra personnel in this case. What is Latin for "didn't quite plan far enough ahead to avoid paying for fifty plane tickets and asking each of those fifty people and make arrangements as if they were going to be gone for three months?"

Some of the fifty were delighted with the news. I felt utter dread. I exchanged looks of disbelief with a fellow avoider of a small boat station.

"Do you think Mr. Johnson would let us stay?" I asked. "There has to be something we could do here so that we wouldn't have to return to our home units."

We brainstormed and approached our would-be supervisor, a reserve warrant officer, to ask if he could think of any reason he would need us over the next few weeks. The thoughtful guy spoke to us with a level of respect we had not experienced since being normal people before bootcamp.

"I'll see what I can do Ms. Caroline and Mr. Brett."

He left to make a phone call in his office and came back with a smile, saying yes, we could stay. My shipmate and I were both approved to help him on documentation within the planning department. He would now supervise demobilization (closing of sites, etc.) and his team was one that actually needed more help than before.

Documentation was right up my alley since I was an avid reader, organizer, and appreciative of a little political gossip. I worked in an air-conditioned office and flipped through papers that came in daily from the response sites and then sorted them by their topical category. Every word on any paper produced from a site had to be archived for the lawsuit against BP.

I started my mornings sipping coffee and reading mayoral complaints and local political gossip. The juiciest correspondence was usually written on sticky notes and the backs of menus, things probably passed around in meetings or stuck on documents that the author intended to keep private. It was early September and because there were elections in November, political rivalries were heating up as blame for economic hardships caused by the oil spill was thrown around. Officials tried to either hide or highlight related corruption, depending on whether or not they were benefiting from it.

"That idiot is going to cost us millions if he keeps letting people make claims."

"Can't trust Mayor XYZ, he's giving out damage claims for votes."

The snippets scratched on documents kept me reading to figure out who was who in these scandals. Some days, I perused financial claims made by people who said they lost their fishing business due to the oil spill; big red scribbles in the margins, written by investigators, corrected a number of claims.

"Claimant lives 175 miles inland. Does *not* own boat, *Merryweather*, as he reported. Vessel *Merryweather*, with registration he listed, sunk in 2002."

BP was doling out cash and everyone wanted a piece.

Culturally, I got a taste of Southern cuisine by skimming the jotted-down lunch orders before I had to sort them into the *unrelated* box. There was lots of Southern cooking and home style menus. Sometimes at lunch we went for seafood because this was probably the last opportunity to eat Gulf seafood before the oil caused real generational damage to the wildlife.

Overall, I read a lot of emails that people probably should not have written, let alone printed. I read, I sorted, and I drank the free diet cokes from the break room. At the end of the day, we reported to the supervisor what we finished and what was left for the next day. It was a simple and glorious existence.

As our work continued, my coworkers' assignments began to expire and most on my team were slowly called back to their home units. It started to feel like *Survivor*, where the day after someone left, we would sadly reminisce about our shipmate who was no longer with us, but also be relieved were still there. Like a forever alliance, upon the request for a shipmate to return home, our faithful supervisor would write a counter request for his teammate to stay, citing that there was more work to do. His counters didn't always work, but for a while some of us were deemed essential to the mission in Alabama.

There certainly was more work to do. As sites and locations continued to close, we had to implement a way for us to receive documents from each of the oil-spill-related offices that were about to thrown away. This meant some friendly liaising with contractors and lawyers' offices. I was happy to integrate a little public interaction into my routine of reading oil-spill documents like they were *People Magazine, Deepwater Horizon Edition.*

One site I had to visit was a lawyer´s office in downtown Mobile. It was close to my hotel, so I walked over before going to work. I wore my heavy dark blue baggy uniform and fifteen-pound black steel toe boots that soaked up the sun's heat. Luckily, we were getting into November and the oppressive Southern summer humidity had subsided. I was content, but tired and a little weighed down. The goal of my visit was to provide the office with guidance on procedures and pick up their related documents.

A young male lawyer greeted me way too eagerly for my morning mood and would not stop staring at me and making comments about women in uniform.

"Women really know how to pull those uniforms off, you sure do."

I rolled my eyes and held my breath up the elevator, thankful that when the doors opened at the top his female colleague was waiting. She cooled his jets, we chatted, and then she waved him away to retrieve the documents for me.

The dude, in his love of women in uniform frenzy, brought two boxes and insisted he carry them for me down the elevator. At the ground floor, I took the boxes, nodded a slight thanks in my innocent and tired *I don't know how to handle this, so I am just going to be polite* manner, and walked back to the hotel to put them in my car and head to the office.

Business went as usual. I gave the team the boxes of documents to sort and worked on my own box. Around four o'clock, my supervisor called me into his office.

"Caroline," he said, calling me by first name, as he usually did, which was a respectful treat I had not yet taken for granted. "That lawyer's office, where are those boxes?"

"Sorted and done! We shipped them off on a pallet an hour ago," I said.

"Mmmhmm, Okay. I got a call from the lawyer you visited today. He accidentally gave you the wrong box; those were related to another client. He wanted to know if he could have it back."

"Uh . . .," I started.

"Not a lot we can do about it," he interrupted, "I'll give him the number to the archives and he can have at it. See you tomorrow."

Thanks to some simple, solid leadership that knew how to define what was our problem and what was someone else's, I did not have to make a three-hour trip to the archives in Louisiana to rummage through papers my team had already rummaged through. I also did not have to meet again with the annoying lawyer. Even better, that annoying lawyer got a 1-800 number to a governmental document storage center instead of my number.

You can't always get what you want, but you get what you need...

The days, weeks, and months passed in Mobile. I walked dogs at the local shelter in my free time, and I had a membership to a fitness center with an abundance of young, fit, Southerners sporting popped polo collars and speaking in their slow, sweet drawls. I also witnessed acts of sheer Alabama dedication to college football.

Whoa! I made a sharp turn into the other toll lane to avoid a car with its backup lights on. *Why is that silver Buick reversing on the toll road!? They are going to get hit!* I watched as the driver stopped, opened her driver's door, leaned out, and retrieved the Alabama car window flag that had fallen as she had approached the toll booth.

Six months on orders was a nice retreat, and eventually my unit requested me back. My optimistic supervisor sent his usual letter to counter and request my extension, but it was denied.

"I hate to see you go," he said, "but I guess it's finally time. Besides the admiral, you're the last active duty person still on orders. That's something to be proud of!"

If it was *Survivor*, I was indeed a winner.

Returning to Montauk in February, though, I wasn't sure I was winning. I can't put together how much more time I spent at the unit, but I eventually got through it and made my way to the Coast Guard's intelligence course.

CHAPTER 12

INTEL SCHOOL

Intelligence training was finally a place where the majority of my peers valued working smarter, not harder.

MOST OF MY ENERGY during intelligence school was spent calculating how late I could leave class and still make it to Virginia Beach to surf before sunset. *It's 2:30 p.m. If I stay late a few minutes, I can skip walking back to the barracks in formation with everyone, which always takes forever, and speed walk back solo. That should get me there by 2:40. I can grab my gear and be on the road by 2:50 p.m.*

Coast Guard intelligence training was based in Yorktown, Virginia and my class spanned from May to August. This was the season for long evenings with just enough time to navigate the Norfolk tunnel and get in the ocean for an hour or two. The waves weren't great, but I was constantly in need of detoxing from living in rank-based submission and subconsciously processing the stress of my experience in Montauk. My first duck dive into the ocean erased the ruminations as well as the uncomfortable Southern summer humidity. Coming back up from under the wave, all I had was the horizon in front of me and the sun setting behind me over the small

Virginia Beach sand dunes. Nothing beat shedding twenty pounds of uniform for a bikini, sandals, and my surfboard.

Discipline-wise, the training was boot camp light:

"Walsh, your shoes are subpar. Taking a point."

Take all the points you want, I'll be using CVS quick shine instead of an hour of actual polishing for the remainder of this course.

Before getting into intel school, I had returned to Montauk from the Deepwater Horizon oil spill. A colleague in Montauk, who I barely knew, had sent me a series of texts about how things had gotten better at the unit. BM2 Twinley, the soon to be registered sexual predator, had assured me the command was less toxic and people were getting along. I returned to find out that was not the case, but there was nothing I could do about it except wait another year and a half to get orders to attend intelligence training. The training and the intel position were what I had intended to be part of since I signed the papers to join the Coast Guard. I thought intel would be an interesting field, consisting of math and strategy balanced with human analysis—similar to my psychology degree.

The waiting list to the school was long because of budget cuts, plus, I'm 90 percent sure the command messed up my initial request for school.

"Hey! Walsh, which school did you want to go to again?"

"Intelligence school, I submitted for it three months ago. Did that not go through?"

"Ummm, it did! Yes it went through, I just forgot. I think I have one more thing for you to sign, uh tomorrow, yes, let's get that together tomorrow."

I was late on an increasingly lengthy list that was sometimes shortened because of limited classes and small class sizes. The list was occasionally static when classes were canceled. The enlisted job rating, *intelligence specialist* was initiated in 2007. Despite the push to prioritize the Coast Guard's security mission, which included intelligence and awareness initiatives, it was a long haul for all of us on the school list who decided to stick to intelligence instead of switching to other schools. I used tuition assistance to help pay for my master's degree that I did on my own time. I finished all but three classes before leaving for the training.

"If you don't get out of here soon, you're going to be Doctor Seaman Walsh," a colleague joked.

"Doing my best to move on." I replied, still waiting for an email about the intel school schedule. The Coast Guard's idea of onboarding enlisted personnel was for new members to spend six months at a traditional unit before attending their job training. This was likely implemented partially to provide experience to new members and partially to have a holding environment as the small organization tried to put people through job training with limited resources. Instead of six months to a year, I had been at my first unit for three years.

Finally, here at intel school. For some reason, I just don't feel like I owe the Coast Guard my shiniest shoes.

My dress shoes were shined enough for any normal office environment, but not for training standards, which caused me to lose points in the class. I didn't really care. We had room inspections and could also lose points if our beds were not tightly tucked with hospital corners folded over. Two weeks into class, my roommates and I started sleeping on top of my bed sheets instead of in them. I was terrible at making the bed each day with such detail. Folding the corners in this way was a specific tucking method that was probably important if we were in a jungle and we needed the rain to not pool in our sheets. Or maybe in a hospital? No matter how much I thought I wanted the physical challenges of intense military training, the Coast Guard fierceness of only losing a few points a day for this stuff was my level. I was okay with not being fully prepared to sleep in the jungle. Or a hospital.

I had one night of heavy drinking and an attempt to drive to DC to visit a friend. This was the first time a hangover with a tinge of still drunkenness got in the way of me doing what I wanted to do.

The night before my trek, I was at a dive bar near base.

"This is great! The music, oh my god! So fun!"

We all thought it was a great spot, until one time we went to the same bar, and the lights were *on* and we realized the place was a dump. The walls looked like they were rotting and it smelled like a dirty bowling alley. That night, though, the lights were off and the booze was flowing. I made it back to the barracks and crashed, then was awakened by an alarm telling me it was time to hit the road to beat traffic to DC. I hopped in the car and started the three-hour drive north. I was tired, my eyes were dry, I sipped my coffee. Three hours.

I reached a stoplight.

Thank God, I can close my eyes for a few minutes.

Even in my state of mind, I knew closing one's eyes while in the driver seat was not a responsible thing to want to do. I pulled over, took out my phone, and found a Holiday Inn a mile away. I had made it twenty-five miles from Yorktown and was unable to reach my destination or return to base.

"You can go out, but you don't have to come back," the Coast Guard's old school motto was ringing true. Except I *would* be coming back to base, just after a sixteen-hour nap in my Holiday Inn suite, the fresh linens cool against my skin. I burrowed into the abundant white pillows for extra darkness. It was noon. Next week, I would have five days of training, then I'd complete the mission to drive to DC the following weekend.

I was getting older, but not yet wise. Once at training, my workout clothes were stolen from the laundry room. I had left them in the dryer for over forty-eight hours because I had gone surfing immediately after class and instead of picking them up that night, and I forgot about them an additional day. I eventually remembered I needed to get the laundry, but it was too late, everything was gone.

Who would want my old soccer shorts with holes in the crotch?

I asked the cleaning staff and the people who ran the lost and found if they had found anything, but no leads. The rest of training

I used my newly learned investigative skills. I discreetly scoured the gym for someone wearing my sports bra.

Her boobs are way too big for my bras. Dammit she's the only female in the whole gym. Who would want my Puma socks?

Given the male-to-female ratios, I was not likely to spot a sports bra. There was a better chance that some dude was sniffing my old undies while putting on lipstick. Too bad there was nothing to sniff because they were already washed and dried.

Even with surfing and drinking antics, I managed to rank number three in the class of about twenty by listening to Lana Del Rey while I studied for an hour each morning on test days. Thanks to her, I had third choice in picking my next unit. The first and second place people picked Colorado and Maryland. Colorado was cool and unique, but no one else wanted Maryland; it seemed like a waste to be in second place for that location.

Joint Interagency Task Force South in Key West, Florida and National Security unit in Hawaii were both open for me. I was pleased I had not wasted time worrying about points and trying create a reflection of my face in my dress shoes.

The surf. Hawaii. Done deal. But I want to get out of this uniform. I want a real, wearing-my-own-clothes, salaried job after two more years of this. What am I going to do after Hawaii? How am I going to visit my new nephew on the East Coast? Time to make the adult choice.

I am not sure where that serious streak came from, perhaps desperation and panic about my uncertain future manifested itself as making a professional choice. I had my sights on being in the best position possible to get out of the Coast Guard once this tour was over. I was not ready to risk being disconnected by thousands of miles from DC, where the jobs were, for Hawaii, where the jobs and family were not. I was putting the waves on hold, but luckily, Key West provided its own adventures.

CHAPTER 13

JOINT TASK FORCE MARGARITAVILLE

I was told to be more aggressive. "Go for the jugular. Go for the jugular and rip it out," Marine Colonel P. said to me at 3:00 a.m. "Um, okay, sir. Going for the jugular," I affirmed as I continued to organize the data on my computer screen.

FOLLOWING THE SAME ROUTE as the yachts of the Hamptons, after intel training, I migrated south from New York to the warm waters of Key West, Florida. My assignment was at the US Southern Command's Joint Interagency Task Force South (JIATFS)—a counternarcotics unit focused on operations in Central and South America's maritime environment. It was weird to be doing serious work for twelve hours while everyone else on the island was getting drunk or fishing . . . or getting drunk *and* fishing, but it provided a decent atmosphere for leadership to not take themselves too seriously.

Key West was also one of those places that was so small that too many people knew who you were—from the homeless man on my street corner to the top leaders at the Task Force.

My mold-filled house was divided into one-bedroom apartments. It was a classic Key West house, with light yellow siding, a white picket fence, and dust and debris everywhere. I was lucky to have Key West's version of a reliable neighbor. She had no health insurance, zero retirement savings, and, if you were on her good side, was a total doll once she had her nightly vodkas.

At one point, I went out of town for training for two weeks and when I returned, she called over for me in her cracking, lifelong cigarette smoker voice. She waved me over, holding her vodka with nearly melted ice in the air.

"Caroline! You know while you were gone, I had to ask a homeless man to stop sleeping on your front porch? Can you believe that? The nerve. I tell you the landlord is *lucky* to have me here . . ." she continued on her usual rant about the landlord, adding a few offensive comments about Jewish people in Miami.

I initially thought that the homeless person's stay on my veranda wasn't a big deal. If I wasn't using the porch, certainly he could. However, as the sweat dripped down my back and my thoughts amplified over my neighbor's anti-Semitic rants, I realized that the reason I should be upset is not because the homeless man used my porch, but that he *knew* that I was gone.

In addition to Key West street stalkers, Key West's Martini Mondays were particularly dangerous. It was easy to have a couple martinis and end up at the barracks on base near the Task Force where fit military men stayed for training. One early Tuesday morning I discovered myself at these barracks. I had to go home to get my uniform before going back on the same base where I currently was, only then, to work.

In most cities, this round trip might take some time, however, on the four by two mile island of Key West, it was a three-minute bike ride. I felt confident handling these simple logistics with brain fog from Martini Monday, now Tuesday. I gathered my belongings and hopped down the outdoor barracks staircase. *Damn, that's evening number three with this guy, practically a six-month relationship by Key West standards.* I was happy enough with slight consistency, but I didn't have time to dwell on it. I took one large inhale of fresh sea air before biking home through the aromas created by stinky beer on hot concrete blended with Tuesday trash pickup fumes. *Paradise.*

I made a left turn off the base and cut the corner into the other lane that was for oncoming traffic, a silver Volvo SUV came into view and screeched to a halt right in front of my bike. My bike and the car stopped about two inches before a collision. I looked up into the windshield to see that it was the Task Force Deputy Director, General Dempsey. I saw him laugh to himself before I gave a quick "sorry" wave, hiding my face, and peeled away on my five-speed, staying out of the oncoming traffic lane for the rest of the ride. I'm sure this happened to him all the time during his early commutes in a town that was full of late-night partiers who had a different kind of morning commute.

Once I got home, I chugged water and threw on my heavy navy-blue uniform with eight-pound black steel toed boots. Nothing says "ready for the office" like clothing that is fire resistant and footwear that makes walking a weight training workout in itself. I had no other responsibilities to tend to, so I grabbed my keys and hopped in the car for a two-minute ride back to base, this time for work. All was good as I cruised through the gates and walked from the ninety-degree parking lot into the air-conditioned hallways. The temperature change gave me a bit of a perk in my step.

I walked into the watch room that was cool and dark, with giant computer monitors displaying maps and maritime routes. General Dempsey was getting briefed on the previous night's operations. Everyone from the director to the weather person were in the room listening to the same brief. That was what people did at the task force. They got their coffee and came to the morning meeting to wait off their hangover, talk to each other about fishing, and be entertained by the night shift's presentation. The night shift desperately wanted to go home to sleep but had to formally pass along information to the day shift crews before they could be released into the sunny inferno of Key West.

General Dempsey was asking a question, but my movement into the room caused him to look at me from the corner of his eye. He got his answer and provided a responding comment, telling the night shift they accomplished a lot that night. He turned to leave the room, accompanied by a Marine colonel and their assistants. Giving me a bit of a one-handed pistol firing gesture, he said "and based on what I saw during my ride in, it looked like Walsh *also* had some accomplishments last night."

I was mortified. I did not even know the General knew who I was. His crew glanced at me and chuckled, putting together what it probably meant. I felt like a kid who thought she was secretly picking her nose behind the couch, only for her parent to yell out in front of the family that it was time to take your finger out of your nose and come to dinner. I walked over to my desk and waited for everyone to leave the watch floor so I could veg out in front of my computer and nurse my hangover, while also aggregating counterdrug intelligence leads, for the next twelve hours.

And so it went with small towns. I had to learn to be the opposite of anonymous with a complete inability to hide my antics even from the highest boss on the island. I did not enjoy it, but I appreciated the transparency the small-town life brought to the workplace. You might say JIATF-S was an early adopter of the idea to take your whole self to work. No one could hide they were a nose picker here.

Overall, morale was good at the Task Force. We had solid leaders who knew how to host harassment-free Christmas parties and let their guard down a little in mostly appropriate ways. Every Friday, the Navy captain in charge of the intelligence personnel would announce which bar he would be at for the evening—half as an invitation and half as a warning not to come into that vicinity if you were stupid drunk. He understood small-town life.

It was nice to feel like a professional and also have a good time with good people, even on the clock. The night shifts were difficult for me but having camaraderie on the watch floor helped us all get through it. One late night conversation was about cell phone plans and which was the best one. I attempted to stay out of the conversation, staring at my computer screen, trying not to engage, but the Marine captain who was the operations officer in charge that night was going around the room demanding to know from everyone what plan they had and how much it cost.

"Walsh! What plan?"

"Family plan?" I responded.

"What's it cost?"

"I don't know, my family pays for it." I said.

The watch floor of about fifteen people in various shades of camouflage uniforms all stared at me, some gasping, some standing up to peer above their computers at who answered that they didn't pay a phone bill.

"Walsh! How old are you? How are your parents still paying for this?"

I shrugged and the captain laughed.

"Man, I can't believe that!" a junior Navy guy snickered, then had a change of heart. "Wait, Walsh, would your parents adopt me?" If anyone else in that room was on the family plan, they were not about to admit it.

That was how the night shifts went on slow nights. Most of the counterdrug action started around two o'clock in the morning, but the shift started at eight the evening before, so there was plenty of time to bullshit before we went for the jugular on the drug traffickers.

CHAPTER 14

JIATF—TRAGIC

*When I tell someone that I have a twin brother I am usually asked,
"what's it like to have a twin?" Uh, I don't know.
What's it like to be born alone?*

"HEY CAROLINE, LET'S HAVE a joke." It was three in the morning, and I was visibly fading. "You can use Google." He was on the watch floor at the computers a level above me where he and the other watch officer sat able to look down at the intelligence specialists and operations specialists.

"I don't need Google, lieutenant! Okay, what did one snowman say to the other snowman?"

"You realize it's pitch-black outside and still eighty degrees? I haven't seen a snowman in five years. I have no idea," he said.

"I smell carrots," I said with as much punch as the late night and my lame joke would let me.

Lieutenant Winter squinted like he wasn't impressed, then burst out in a genuine laugh.

"I like it! You hear that, Garrett?" he elbowed the officer next to him, "I smell carrots," he looked at the clock above the giant screens, "Alright four more hours of this, who has a joke to top the snowman joke?"

Lieutenant Winter was a Navy lieutenant, mid-thirties—a cheeky guy with short, blond buzzed hair and a slim runner's body. He was a favorite of many because of his dry humor and concern for the people who worked below him. If something went wrong in a brief, from a junior person not having an answer, to a wrong PowerPoint slide, he would take the heat even if it was someone else's fault. His sacrificial style of leadership stood out compared to other supervisors, who when asked a question, would dodge it and look at the junior personnel to come up with an explanation on the spot. The other supervisors exemplified the phrase of *throwing someone under the bus*, whereas Lieutenant Winter gladly stepped out in front of that bus, perhaps sometimes with less concern than considered normal. He was a complicated guy, but a good leader.

This lieutenant was cool, was a good person, took shifts for people when needed, was kind, and was goofy. He had worked on a submarine before being assigned to this unit. He possibly drank occasionally, but he was insanely sharp, and from what I saw, he was not the kind of person you'd label as an alcoholic or even a functioning alcoholic.

The day he took his life I was leaving the night shift and he was supposed to be oncoming for the day shift, but he didn't show up. This was not like him, so people called, then waited. He still didn't arrive so one of the day shift personnel was sent to go to his house and that is where they found him. He had shot himself.

Everyone was shocked, but in hindsight, it wasn't completely blindsiding. At his funeral and surrounding comments, the command blamed alcohol abuse. They did not acknowledge that Lieutenant Winter was a few weeks from leaving the Navy and he did not have a plan of what he was going to do or where he was going to go once he left the service. They did not acknowledge his strained relationship with the Mormon church in which he grew up. They did not talk about his time on submarines, which are manned by a tight-knit community that experienced enough suicides that in 2006, the commander of Naval submarine forces sent a memo to his leaders to pay special attention to preventing suicides. From Connecticut to Hawaii, it seemed like that force regularly dealt with a lot of suicides, having three occur within six months in 2021. Lieutenant Winter also had a preference for night shifts, seeming to feel better avoiding a life of weekends and days free. Maybe alcohol lowered his inhibitions, but I do not believe his pain and loss of faith in the future came *from* drinking. We will never know, but, perhaps part of his struggle came from not having a path forward, and not having strong ties with his family or with others outside the Navy world. If those in senior positions had been concerned about his plan for the future, they didn't seem to take any action. On one hand, he was a grown adult; on the other, by serving in the military he became disconnected from other possible paths and the military owed him help in reconnecting. He was about to end his job at the unit in a few weeks yet wasn't even able to answer the question of whether he was going to extend his lease in Key West or leave for another place.

Lieutenant Winter was an intense and caring dude. He was a man in a leadership position who I never felt threatened by, and who respected me as a person, going out of his way to call me and others by our first names once the military leadership left for the day. Now, he was another statistic to the military, another example of the stress, fear, and disorienting experience of leaving military service. It's fear-inducing enough to leave when you have a support network and a plan, things that many service members lack after being in military world with all military people. Many of those same people who stay in the service do not know the jobs of the outside world. They would only instill more fear in you because they also have yet to venture out.

"Yeah, you'll be back," a disgruntled fifteen-year military member would say to those leaving the service. He had come back in the service himself, after trying to make it in the civilian world, and knew that the transition process was disheartening. It left a lot of people struggling, like they were drowning and desperately reaching to grasp whatever lifeline was closest in order to save themselves.

My own transition was not easy. I had intelligence experience that had related civilian jobs, but it was nearly impossible to line up a job with my end of enlistment date. I was stationed in Key West, which was 100 miles from the closest big city, Miami, and a plane ride from the city I wanted to be in, Washington, DC. Most organizations did not do virtual interviews, and if I even got to that, most took one look at my Florida address and dismissed my application. Even using a friend's DC address, I was told they did not hire that far out or needed someone available to interview next week.

"I don't know what to do," I would tell friends and family, but they didn't know this line of work. They didn't know what requirements existed for certain jobs and what I might qualify for; they were there for support, but I was on my own, career-wise.

I realized it was going to be impossible to secure any job prior to leaving the unit and moving to DC. I needed to commit to leaving the Coast Guard with or without a job.

"What are you going to do in DC?" the movers asked as I sat poolside in the backyard of my moldy Key West apartment and sipped tequila.

"Not sure, just pretty sure there's nothing for me here," I replied.

I lived with my sister outside of DC for six months, teaching art classes, interviewing, and tutoring seventh-grade math, before landing a full-time job. The only reason I knew of the job was because I was in contact with a reservist from the Key West unit who connected me with her friend. That friend connected me with a friend running a contracting company that recently won a contract with the Department of Homeland Security. I got something. It wasn't the job I wanted, and the salary was so low I had to reach into savings to pay rent, but after six months of feeling worthless and like I'd be stuck and jobless forever, I took the job.

Regardless of the real reasons behind his suicide, that we will never know, Lieutenant Winter spurred my passion for nonprofits and programs that support all veterans in progressing through the transition to civilian life. Not only is the military's transition program not enough, but the Department of Veterans Affairs is overwhelmed with people with serious issues to be able to care for the rest who are just struggling to figure out what's next.

After his death, things went on. The task force recovered, people welcomed babies with baby showers and we threw margarita-filled birthday parties. The memory of him lingered though, and every formal event reminded me of his funeral.

"Lieutenant Smith," the funeral had reached the point of the *last roll call* and began by calling out to the unit members present.

"Present," Smith responded.

"Lieutenant Presley."

"Present," Presley responded.

"Lieutenant Winters," the person directing the funeral paused, "Lieutenant Winters," he repeated before calling for the third and last time before the heart wrenching silence, "Lieutenant Winters."

CHAPTER 15

SWIMMING AND OTHER HAZARDS OF KEY WEST

My friend got her boobs done and gave me all her old bathing suit tops. I was feeling really good about it, until I wasn't.

"COME SWIM, YOU'LL FEEL better."

I was coming off a series of night shifts and the sun was starting to dart in through the cracks between my black out curtains.

"Okay, okay. Give me ten minutes to get myself together." I sighed in an attempt to try to get started, rolled to the side, and put my feet on the floor.

Ugh, it's humid.

It was November in Key West. The Caribbean-like ocean water had finally cooled to a tolerable temperature for open water swimming. I opened my drawer with all my swim gear and grabbed the turquoise goggles, pink swim cap, and new triathlon bikini that would actually stay in place. I groggily went outside, unlocked my bike, and shuffled with it through the white fence that surrounded the yard. I threw on my small backpack of gear, got on my bike, and headed to our spot.

"What do you want to do? The usual?" I asked Jen as we looked out at the White Street pier that was our normal practicing grounds.

"Yeah, maybe a little extra if you're up for it," she said, then peered behind her to the sandy palm trees. "Wait a second," she squinted and stared at a seemingly homeless man who was sitting under the tree. Like many cities, Key West was full of homeless people. Here, they made different parts of the island their regular territory. I had seen this guy before. He was always looking out at the swimmers and families that would gather and play at this particular beach location.

"Hang on a sec." She started walking over to him. In addition to being a hot Latina fitness model and triathlete with long dark hair and every muscle perfectly defined, Jen was a cop who had recently moved into detective work. She had all kinds of responsibilities on the island from managing traffic during drunken parades to investigating atrocious homicides, like a beheading at a local retirement home.

"Ken," she said firmly, "you skipped your last check in. If I don't see you later today at the station, you are going to be in serious trouble. I don't think you're supposed to be hanging out here either." Jen pointed for him to leave. He gathered his things and obliged.

"What was that about?" I asked as I put my swim goggles over my cap.

"Sexual predator," she said, "skipped out on his last parole check in."

"Gross."

"Yeah, real gross. Not sure where he's supposed to be exactly, not near kids or schools, but this island is four by two miles so it's tricky."

Ugh. It hit me that this guy was always here watching me and others in our bathing suits having no idea what weird shit he was creating in his mind, some of which he had obviously followed through on.

"Let's go."

We walked to the end of the pier and eased ourselves into the relatively chilly water.

"Oh girl! Your nips are gonna freeze in this!" Jen joked as she took a breath and went all the way under. I jumped in after her. The salty cool water felt good on my drained body and mind. We treaded water and made a plan.

"Three laps to that buoy and back. I'm going to focus on my form, but you can go ahead if you need to," she said.

"I am not in any shape to pull ahead of you," I responded. "Okay, ready?"

"Ready."

And off we went. Smooth swimming strokes with the sun above us and the clear water down to the sand below. We got into our meditative rhythms and before we knew it, we reached the buoy and treaded water again.

"How was that?" she asked.

"Great! Good pace," I said with more energy than I had in the last week.

"Girl, okay, I know I said three laps and training and all that, but I gotta catch you up on the gossip!"

We chatted as we kept ourselves afloat. It was our usual pattern, get ourselves going, then talk boys and drama as we commented about how treading water had to be great for our abdominals.

"And *then* that mother f-er said I was the lazy one! Can you believe that?" Jen ranted. "Alright, enough! Race you back to the pier!"

We picked up speed on this round, hit the pier, and did our version of an open water kickflip back to the buoy. Arms straight out, I tried to see how far I could glide before I had to paddle again. Moving through the cool water brought me back to life.

We reached the buoy again. Jen stood up where we stopped in about four feet of water. She was out of breath from the sprints and so was I. Instead of our usual treading water, I went to stand too. I put my face in the water and looked down to the light blue tinted sand to where I was going to put my feet. I didn't want to step on coral or anything sharp.

"And then," Jen continued as I relaxed and put one foot down.

"*Ah*! *What the fuck*!," I screamed.

Jen stopped talking. "Oh my god. Oh my god," I said a little calmer, but still panicked.

"We have to go in," I said sternly, "we have to go in, *now*. I think something bit me." The pain was starting to hit me and I was afraid my foot was bleeding.

I started swimming directly to the shore at a quick pace and Jen followed. When we reached the sand, she got closer to me, "What happened? Let me help you," she said.

"It's my foot," I explained, "Fuck! My foot." I clenched my teeth, "I put my foot down and I think a shark or something took a bite. It was quick, but strong."

She helped me hobble to the sand where I could sit and she could look at what happened. Blood was oozing slowly from the top of my foot. She examined it, lifting my foot and trying to see what she could do to help.

"Girl, you got stabbed," she said, "that's a stingray wound. There's nothing on the bottom of your foot, nothing bit you, but some giant stingray sure was pissed. We've got to get you to the ER so they can clean it."

"Ugh, I can't drive like this!"

"I know, I know. Don't worry, I've got the squad car. I'll take you and can go into work later."

We got in the car and she hit the siren once as we took off. Jen grinned at me, trying to get my mind off the pain, "you're a VIP. Don't worry, you'll be okay."

"Owwwwww," I put my head back and tried to take deep breaths. It felt like someone had jabbed me with a knife and then somehow made it feel worse and stinging.

The Key West ER was quiet. Most of their business was from late night partiers and by now it was eleven in the morning and the madness had cleared. An ultra tan doctor who wore a Hawaiian shirt under his white coat greeted me as I sat down in my assigned room. My wet shorts and top melted the paper that lined the reclining seat.

"Okay! We've got a stingray, so nothing unusual here," the doctor said as he started poking around at my foot and wound. "This guy got you good!" He grabbed the syringes he had brought in. "We're going to numb the area. I need to make sure the stinger is all the way out. Sometimes it stays in and then we have to move to surgery."

"Surgery?" I looked at Jen.

"Don't worry, that's not common," she assured me.

"Jeeeen," I whined, "I'm supposed to get out of here and go to Virginia for training tomorrow. I just want a break from this island." I started to cry. I was in pain, I was worried, I was mad at myself for standing in the water. I never stood, for this exact reason.

The doctor continued to inspect my foot, but I could no longer feel his fingers on the wound. Still, watching him dig into my skin made me nauseous. I looked up at the ceiling and away from the scene.

"Good news, no stinger!" He said very jolly, like this incident was the least of his worries. "We'll get you some pain meds, an antibiotic, and have you had your tetanus shot recently?"

"Probably, I think I got stuck with everything in bootcamp," I responded. He handed me the first round of pain pills and I relaxed, accepted the crutches he offered, and hobbled off with Jen back to the cop car.

"You have to go to work?" I asked her.

"No, I'm good, called in until the evening."

"What? You didn't have to do that! Jen, thank you."

"No problem, girl. Let's go get sushi and show those marine animals who is boss in the animal kingdom!"

CHAPTER 16

JIATF—DATING

*You almost have to drink if you live in Key West, otherwise,
you'll realize your evening is the same as the last three
hundred and sixty-five.*

AS IF KEY WEST work and ocean life were not dangerous enough, the small island of military men (who were temporary), bachelor party bros (whose buddies all took off their wedding rings by bar number two), and the crews of young alcoholics (who ran the tourist activities), each brought their own risks. I had been in Key West for a year, and I had tried it all. I was probably initially too open when it came to dating. Some people have a list of things their partner *must have* and a list of definite *no-goes*. My internal calculation started as a rhetorical *why not!* It was rhetorical because there were usually plenty of reasons why not.

"Hey . . . hey. Um, hey," I reached down to tap his shoulder. No response. I felt his breath on my inner thighs, so I knew he wasn't dead. I sat up in my bed and pulled my legs back together in a tuck, then pivoted away from his face. "Matt?" He made a sound. A snort, then a snore. He was asleep. He fell asleep in the middle of some light afternoon foreplay. Matt was a former Marine who had moved back to Key West because he didn't know what else to do after he left active duty. He worked at the bars at night and despite his alcohol-induced narcolepsy, also worked as a lifeguard at a hotel pool. We had just gotten back to my house after lounging that morning at one of the pools he had access to; he had started drinking before I got there.

I knew he had a drinking problem, but damn, it's two in the afternoon. Did I not keep up with his drinking? I am buzzed, but I'm not about to pass out.

I got up and went about my chores around the house while Matt snored at the foot of my bed. It didn't even seem weird; I was used to what it meant to live in Key West. Jacob was another Key West guy I just never could sync up with.

"What are you doing?" Jacob texted one day.

"Just got off work." I replied. It was nine in the morning and I had the night shift that week.

"Brunch?"

He's such a nice guy, but brunch with him and his five hung-over friends? I need to sleep.

"I would but I'm exhausted! Will be up later this afternoon," I replied. And I would be, but I would be hitting the gym in preparation to push through another twelve hours of overnight work.

"Cool, we'll grab coffee," he said, but we would not, he would be on a sunset party boat with his buddies.

My favorite and longest lasting *text* relationship happened when innocent flirting turned into me unknowingly signing up for regular dick-pic distribution. I didn't exactly unsubscribe right away. It only cost me an occasional emoji response to confirm that I was still an avid reader of his publication.

Years later, I would find out that all the nonsense could have been prevented if one of my supervisors had not cockblocked me from going out with a respectable active-duty officer attached to the task force. Apparently, the nice young man had asked the other Coast Guard intelligence specialist, who was my age, but two ranks above, if it would be okay to ask me out. Instead of saving me from multiple years of my own efforts to counter island loneliness, my Coast Guard colleague went full regulations and advised him that because he was an officer and I was enlisted, it would not be inappropriate. I would often see the officer out at the bars, but he always seemed to keep his distance. *Thanks, shipmate.*

I suppose Key West was not 100 percent the responsible choice, especially when it came to finding a mate, but the work was satisfying. I was young enough to play around on my days off and still have the energy to get things done when I was at work. Even with dating, swimming, and other antics, I developed solid relationships with high-level and well-connected people at the task force. I worked, I traveled, I met with people from other nations and improved my Spanish skills to reach the Department of Defense *translator* level. I would not call myself a translator, but it didn't hurt the resume.

CHAPTER 17

I'M AN IDIOT,
BUT SO ARE YOU

*"So, one Coast Guard unit's patch has a shark, another
has a dolphin, and one has a trident. But surely this one
can't be a shrimp riding a seahorse."*

"Too much attention to detail, Walsh."

ONE PROBLEM WITH JOINING the military after college and
a comfortable middle-class life is that you go from one bubble to
another without being in the real world to know how health insurance
works. The cost of health care came up once in a while in my twenties,
but I never had the chance to understand what the cost problem was.
Growing up, our prescriptions were never more than fifteen dollars.
I had heard the word *copay* but had no idea what it meant.

With this perspective, I was a few years into the Coast Guard
and starting to have some health problems. After talking to a doctor
friend and doing some research, I was pretty sure I had an issue that
blood work could diagnose so looked up the details to figure out
what blood tests I should get.

I went to the Coast Guard doctor at the Coast Guard base in Key West. This was separate from the Joint Task Force where I worked. I hated going to the Coast Guard base for anything since the one time I went to the doctor with a 103-degree fever and was told I had to be in uniform to be seen. I had deliberately changed into my Coast-Guard-issued fitness gear because I figured that would be sufficient. No one with a 103 fever has the energy to change into a dark blue, twenty-pound, heat-holding uniform, especially when the Key West sun is raging at 95 degrees with 80 percent humidity. I felt like this medical unit was always hassling me and thus, like others at the Joint Task Force, I avoided it except when absolutely needed.

But this visit was necessary. I had been feeling like shit for a while, even when I stopped drinking and continued exercising regularly. I was pretty sure it was thyroid-related given the symptoms and family history. I told the doctor my symptoms and he did not appreciate that I suggested what I thought it could be. I was just a dumb enlisted person to him. He would be the one doing the diagnosis.

"Are you single?" he asked.

"Uh, yeah?" I responded, "right now, yeah."

"Uh huh," he nodded arrogantly, suggesting that what I was experiencing was all in my head.

I made another appointment after he gave me his bullshit advice. This time he agreed to the blood testing. The doctor, with his balding black hair and stupid dark mustache, gave me a sheet of paper to take to the testing facility off base.

Is he single? Maybe he *is the one who hasn't gotten laid in a while.*

He had checked off about two things on the list of items to test. I went home to change out of my uniform, checked my research, and checked off a few more items that were related to what I thought I might be experiencing. I went to the local lab and had my blood drawn without a problem.

I had another appointment to go over the results from the blood work. First, the health service specialist (HS2) came in the room. He was short and stocky, with wiry glasses. HS2 was essentially my peer who had a couple months of Coast Guard training on health issues like I had a couple months of Coast Guard training on intelligence work. Although I would rather not have him looking into my personal medical stuff, he took a look at the results while in the room with me and gave me a questioning look. He told me to wait, he had to go get the doctor.

The doctor came in super mad and, like a trusty evil sidekick, HS2 became equally pissed off and ready to lay it on me. The HS2 shook the paper at me while doctor pointed to it and yelled, "who marked to have all these tests done?"

"I did," I replied, confused by all the emotion. "I looked it up and these would also be helpful. I didn't feel like coming back so I checked them off myself."

"This is fraud! You just cost the Coast Guard thousands of dollars!"

He pointed me toward the door to leave. I think he needed to cool down. I was upset with the word fraud. I had just gotten my security clearance and was sure that was not going to be a good look. I walked across the hot black pavement to my car and went home.

The next day at work, I got called into my supervisor's office and he asked me to explain what happened. Commander Riddles looked like he would be a goofy guy who you could make jokes with. He was very tall, with a wave of blond hair that he whipped back with mousse. He never acted like a goof, though, despite his lanky looks. After talking to him previously, I knew I could not speak too freely and usually ended our discussions with a "yes, sir."

"Walsh, the doctor wants an investigation. Intelligence Specialist First Class (IS1) Towns will conduct it. You are to tell her your story and she'll talk to the doctor and HS2 and make a recommendation to me based on her interviews."

"Commander Riddles, would it be possible for me to just pay what I owe for the tests and we do not have to go through all of this?" I asked.

He paused as he looked down and held his chin in one hand, tapping his pointer finger on his nose in contemplation. He looked as if he wanted to say yes. He let out a sigh. "No."

IS1 Towns was a Navy IS1 who had been in for over fifteen years. To say she was salty was an understatement. She was salt *encrusted* and rightfully so. On top of that, she was a take-no-shit-from-anyone Mississippi woman who was nearly six feet tall and not afraid to stand up straight. I admired and feared her at the same time. We had our disagreements though, mostly based on our generational differences, and she was not really a huge fan of mine.

I told my medical story to IS1. She kept a straight face and stuck to the questions without any chitchat.

"Did the doctor express that he wanted you to have all these tests?"

"No, he only checked two and I checked the others."

"So, you took it upon yourself. Are you a medical doctor?" she continued to grill me.

"No."

"Do you have any medical training?"

"No. I mean, I studied neuroscience in college, but I guess that's not training."

"Did any of the tests you checked off have abnormal results?"

"Yes, one of them was high," I said. She asked a few more questions and took notes. Without any indication of what she thought, she dismissed me.

I went home and the gravity of what was happening sunk in. I just got investigated for something that the doctor labeled as *defrauding the government.*

This can't be happening. I made it through three years of miserable Coast Guard life to get to this position. I have my security clearance. I'm at a unit with decent people. And now, it's all going to get taken away. I hated the doctor. He was an ego-tripping dick and so was his little weasel sidekick HS2. *Why would someone like that want to*

ruin me? What happened to do no harm? *The Montauk curse is true.*
I was doomed from the beginning. One idiot mistake of mine and it's
all going to get taken away.

I cycled through the stages of grief, wondered if I should contact
a lawyer, and accepted that the realistic worst-case scenario was that
my security clearance level would be reduced because I would be
deemed untrustworthy. I then would have to transfer to a different
unit with less sensitive collection methods. It would probably be
at an all-Coast Guard unit. I would be spending my days counting
fishermen's catches or doing data entry-style intel. Everyone would
be annoying, and I would have to start all over with everything.

I had another meeting with Commander Riddles after he met
with IS1 following her interviews.

"Well . . . Walsh," he laid down a few documents on the desk.
"What we have here is a conclusion! I'll need you to sign here," he
pointed, "here and here to acknowledge the receipt of this document.
You are receiving a warning, and this is official documentation of this
incident that will remain in your records. You must understand that
you are not to do this again. Don't do this again, Walsh."

I almost cried. I bit my cheek to keep the tears of relief from
spilling out and thanked him. My career was not ruined. It might
even be looked over when I applied to officer candidate school. The
only punishment was the fear and worry I had already done to myself.

"Don't thank me, Walsh. It was IS1 who turned things around.
She did not like that one of the tests you checked was abnormal and
used that to show that it was possible the doctor was negligent, and
he backed down."

I walked out to the watch floor to find IS1. She was sitting on the
upper level by herself with a computer in front of her.

"Um, IS1. Sorry to interrupt. I just wanted to thank you for
conducting the investigation fairly," I looked down at the blue and
black speckled floor, again trying not to cry.

"Walsh, don't you worry about a thing," her Mississippi accent slipped out. She continued firmly. "You've got a long career ahead of you. This will be out of your file in a few years," she paused. "Don't make me have to do anything like this again!" She let her Southern accent fly and gave me a wink.

A woman who did not like me at all saved my career from an idiot doctor who would have felt joy in taking it all away. I still couldn't believe the world I was living in.

CHAPTER 18

WHAT IS IT LIKE TO BE A WOMAN IN THE MILITARY?

In 1881, Ida Lewis was first woman awarded the Coast Guard's Gold Lifesaving Medal. I wonder if she too had to deal with her unit only buying her extra small mechanic coveralls.

"I FEEL REALLY UNCOMFORTABLE right now," my boyfriend said to me.

We were volunteering at a Girl Scout camp for the day. He had just walked with his lunch tray from the food line to the table to sit with me. Visibly uncomfortable and slightly unsure of himself, he looked down as he walked. Dozens of girls and women filled the cafeteria tables in a large gym-like room. They were energetic and excited to be at a camp full of other women. As the only male, my companion couldn't escape being different from the crowd. Did they think he was attractive? Were they just curious? If he smiled, would they get the wrong impression? He was beginning to feel overwhelmed being the object of so many female glances.

"That's how I feel *every day,*" I replied.

Once, I was in a closed brick room with a Marine sociopath in charge of our small Coast Guard group. He looked around to make sure everyone was ready, then pressed the button to release the tear gas, clearly enjoying his knowledge of the pain we were all about to face. Our masks were on to start, I heard the gas release and felt a burning sensation on my face like a sunburn so bad it would turn purple. My nose swelled with liquid snot, my eyes burned and blinked more and more rapidly in pain, trying to rid themselves of the invasive gas. I could hardly breath. I looked around to see if anyone else was struggling. If they were, they did not show it. *Oh my god, this sucks*! I could hardly stand still. I felt like I was drowning, and no one saw that I needed help.

"*Now*," the marine gave the signal to break the seal on the masks to let the gas in. I pulled my mask out an inch and waited for the increased pain, but it didn't come. Just more snot and I could barely breath. After breaking the seal, as part of the training, I then sealed the mask back to my face. We were supposed to clear out the gas with a giant breath. Breathing in hot stingy air, I tried to blow it out, but nothing cleared. I tried again, but still the air stung without relief. *I can't breath, what the fuck.* I gave the signal I was leaving and walked out the door, trying to hide my frustrated panic.

The sun was out, I ripped off the gas mask as an instructor waiting outside approached me. Snot covered my face and kept coming out of everywhere possible. My nose ran, my eyes dripped, my mouth salivated, all attempting to eliminate what I had been breathing in.

"Walsh, what happened?"

"I don't know! It fucking burned the whole time. I hate this. Why do I suck at this?" I spit everywhere as I was talking, and he handed me a bottle of water.

"The whole time?" he asked.

"Yeah, the gas released and two seconds later I wanted to die because of the burning."

"Walsh, that means your mask wasn't working; you're supposed to be fine until you break the seal. The challenge is to clear the gas, not to be in the gas cloud for eight minutes. Give me your mask."

I handed it to him, he doused it in water and then inspected it.

"Nothing is wrong with the mask," he said. "Here." He handed it back to me. "Put it on and let's see."

By now I had cleared the snot from my face and everyone else walked out from the building, their faces red and dripping. I put the mask on for the instructor to check.

"I see, Walsh, it isn't sealing because your bun is in the way. Your hair, you need to change it so the mask can seal."

"My hair!" My face was still burning, which contributed to me being livid. "This is how I'm supposed to wear it! Low bun, no ponytail, per regulations. What do you want me to do?"

"I don't know," he said.

"You're telling me that in real life, outside of training, there's going to be tear gas or something worse, released and I'm going to stop and redo my hair real quick? Just a couple mustard gas blisters," I said sarcastically, "before putting on the mask?"

"Well, the Coast Guard is a little behind," he explained, "the female Marines are using a mask that has a hairnet style closure on the back instead of a strap, it lets the mask seal without anything getting in the way. So, yeah, unless you get that, you'll be breathing in anthrax spores until you can undo your hair and redo it so the mask seals. Guys have the same problem if they have beards, except I guess we shave our beards. You could shave your head," he offered.

Not only was I trying to figure out the intentions of men glancing or staring at me day after day, but also, unless the Coast Guard invested in buying masks that fit the hair regulations they created for women, I would be out of luck in the case of any biological or chemical attack. Was I supposed to make a scene and demand that the Coast Guard buy appropriate masks for women? Probably. Would that provide some men another reason to justify their view that having women in the military was a nuisance? Probably. That is part of what it is like to be a woman in the military.

"Walsh! You're the only female in the class, would you like to come up to let us demonstrate the search procedures?"

All eyes looked to me. It was a law enforcement class of about ten young, enlisted men from other units who I had never met before. Half were scraggly, barely twenty-year-old kids and the other half were the buff type who couldn't wait for class to be over so they could hit the weight room. The three instructors had only a few more years of experience than the rest of the class.

"Yes?" I answered uncertainly. I did not have time to think through what this was going to be like. The instructor was right, I was the only female, so why shouldn't I volunteer for the demo? I walked up in front of my classmates, who were standing in a line in the basketball court turned training room.

"Widen your stance," he said to me in the new age law enforcement language that had realized *spread your legs* was offensive. "Now, for a female, you keep your hand straight as you run it under their chest and on the sides of the breasts to check for contraband hidden in their bra."

He put his hand on the side of my boob and ran it along the edge. Then he pivoted his hand flat and ran it underneath my boob. "You want to use the back of your hand against the breast to avoid women accusing you of cupping them," he made a cupping shape with his hands in front my chest.

All eyes were still on me, plus now, specifically on my chest and his hand nearly cupping me. I held my breath. One of the guys grinned. I looked at the shiny wood paneled floor.

This was a bad idea.

"And then for the groin, again, straight hand and run it along the leg up to the pubic area."

His hand hit my groin. My legs were shaking from being used as a dummy in front of a bunch of guys I did not know and at least one was enjoying the show. The instructor stood up from the groin procedure. "And then, if they are on the ground, you will do the following search procedures as they lay on their back with their legs in a wide position," he looked at my face. Flushed, uncertain, nervous. "Actually, Walsh, you can sit down now."

"Thanks," I managed to mutter. I walked back to stand with the class.

Four more days of this.

The instructors meant well and emphasized professionalism. They saw having a female in the class as an opportunity, which was a decent intention. However, not only did the impact not match their intent, but at this point in my Coast Guard experience, becoming the live dummy on body searches was not the opportunity I was looking for.

CHAPTER 19

TIME TO GO

Coast Guard Captain Healy, of the late 1800s, was famous for his grit in Alaska's arctic conditions, and cited for his forty-hour watches on his vessel while wet, cold, and hungry. I liked the outdoors and all, but maybe it was time to enjoy it with my own agenda.

BEING READY TO LEAVE the active-duty experience without looking back was like an incident when I was six years old and begged my mom to let me go on a swinging ship ride by myself. I had watched the giant ship, outfitted with Peter Pan pirate knockoff decorations, swing back and forth, sailing like a pendulum. The confident Captain Hook-like character was on the bow, looking out with his telescope. The chubby and clumsy Smee-like character was a mannequin lower on the ship made to look like he was struggling to keep steady with the rocking of the boat. His bucket of water was mid-spill and he his mop was about to fly out of his hands. The ride looked fun and exciting.

"Please, Mom! Please, I want to go," I pleaded.

"Okay, let's go," she replied.

"No, by myself. I want go by myself."

She waited with me in line, holding my hand. The gate opened to let the new riders on, and I left her hand dangling to leap up the steps to find a good seat. I pulled down the safety harness, built for adults, and waved to her before I went about my business. I looked around at the people next to me then lost interest in them and watched the birds dart between the pine trees behind the ride.

The ship's movement began, a gentle swing forward, a smooth sail back. Then again, forward and back. The third time, the force increased and the ship swung *double* the height it had gone the last two swings. My back was parallel to the ground as I looked straight up at the sky. Next, it violently swung itself back at equal height. I was looking straight down at the concrete. I felt my small body shift in the harness, gravity pulled me down and my back no longer touched the seat behind me. I was jolted back and forth between the seat and harness over the next few swings. This was not the excitement I wanted. I shrieked and then verbalized my feelings.

"*Get me off this stupid ride!*" I yelled as we swung forward again forcefully and my body hit the back of the seat again.

"*I want off this stupid ride!*" I continued yelling to no one in particular during the backwards swing. I released additional variations of loud complaints into the sky for each of the subsequent movements. I had no idea if anyone could hear me. I thought I was as high as the clouds and yelling into the air about how miserable I was and ready for it to stop as soon as possible.

When the ride stopped, I unstrapped my harness, hopped out of my seat, and made my way to the exit, stomping down the metal walkway to the gate where my mom was waiting and holding in laughter.

"Did you have a good time?"

"I *hate* that ride, it's so *stupid*! It went *too high*! I'm too small; I almost fell out! I never want to go on it *again*!" I summarized.

"I heard," she replied, and we walked away to the next ride that piqued my interest.

My Coast Guard ride had swung me too high, and I was ready to get off. I held in my thoughts on its stupidity because I knew others around me would be staying in and they loved the ride. They were built for the harness and whiplash motions. I accepted that I was not.

What would I do if I signed up for four more years and the next unit was as toxic as the first? I wouldn't be able to fake any professionalism. That would not end well for me.

Knowing I would not be able to hold in my screaming inner child, I ended on a good note. Or at least a decent one.

I left active duty and signed up for an immediate transition to the Coast Guard Reserves. I was moving to live with my sister outside of Washington, DC and was assigned to a reserve unit in Virginia Beach.

Maybe I'll get some waves there, I thought, after spending the last two years in the flat Key West Caribbean waters.

I also applied for Reserve Officer Candidate Indoctrination (ROCI). I had never gotten into the active-duty officer candidate school with its budget cuts and my lack of experience. I had the undergraduate degree to meet its qualification, but my lack of higher rank and ebbing faith in the career path left me overlooked by the program. I still wanted to lead, though—once I had some rest. I wanted to do things the right way for people, especially female Coast Guard members. I wanted them to be part of the team, to feel the safety and belonging I had never fully felt.

Unfortunately, as part of the officer application, I needed a Coast Guard medical exam before I left Key West. I had to see the disgruntled doctor and his trusty sidekick again.

These motherfuckers.

It pained me to dial to make an appointment. I felt even more pain and resistance as I entered the medical office the next week. I opened the light teal hospital-style door to their stark white office.

"I'm here for my appointment," I said flatly.

HS2 looked up, "Okay," he said. "Just wait over there." He waived me off impatiently, like he had very important things to do.

When I was finally called in, the doctor and HS2 were both in the room with me.

"What are we doing for you today?" the doctor asked while flipping through an irrelevant clipboard and avoiding eye contact. I had heard through office gossip that his attempt to get me in trouble for the extra bloodwork resulted in him getting *himself* in trouble.

"I need this physical for my officer candidate school application," I said as I handed him the forms.

"Officer candidate school? But you're only recently an E-5." He was the doctor and obviously all-knowing.

"Um, I have a bachelor's degree. And I just finished my master's," I replied, with as little emotion as possible. I just wanted the paperwork finished.

It took a moment before the doctor said, "Well, IS2 Walsh, congratulations," his stern frown relaxed into the face of someone who didn't hate me. "Alright, let's get started. We'll have this ready for you in no time." His sidekick followed suit and stopped glaring at me.

It was a quick appointment. I got the exam and signatures I needed. As I was leaving, I signed out with HS2 at the front desk.

"Good luck, IS2!" he said to me. "We'll see you again in the field, I'm sure."

I hope not.

"Thanks, man," I replied.

Did they really just treat me like a human being because I might be an officer in the next year? The answer was probably only going to piss me off.

I left that base for good and went home to get my house packed up for my move to DC. I arrived ready to charge into a civilian career. I found some time to rest as well. I went to a friend's wedding without having to ask anyone for approval to travel. I slept in my sister's basement guest room that was quiet and stayed dark past eight o'clock. It was a respite from the Key West sunlight's early morning burn and the hollering roosters of my neighbors. I took my time in the mornings to stretch and play games with my nephew before starting the day. I taught art classes, English lessons, and tutored seventh-grade math that was beyond my teaching level. When I was feeling disconnected and losing faith that I would ever find a job, my one weekend a month reserve duty brought me back to good old Southern Virginia.

CHAPTER 20

SOUTHERN VIRGINIA PART II—VA BEACH

Military duty should be mandatory for all citizens so that I don't have to deal with more guys who feel ashamed that they never joined.

AFTER SOUTHERN VIRGINIA ROUND one of intel school in Yorktown, Virginia, I was off to my new enlisted reserve responsibilities on the Dam Neck Naval base in Virginia Beach. The unit was MIFC LANT (Maritime Intelligence Fusion Center — Atlantic). It sounded official enough. After being at the joint task force in Key West, it was time to learn what Coast Guard intelligence culture was all about.

Dam Neck is a known Navy SEAL base, but also has other random buildings on it, like ours. We weren't doing anything related to any of their stuff, but it didn't stop Coast Guard dudes from thinking they were super cool being on that base. I'm sure they picked up tons of chicks on the weekends saying they worked on Dam Neck and pretending they had to be all hush-hush about their intel work. *Good for them.* Even a decent guy I worked with on base would name drop surfing with his SEAL pals.

"Yeah, it was so great, they are SEALS, you know, my SEAL buddies, who I surf with, the SEAL guys. SEAL. Did I mention I sometimes surf with Navy SEALS?"

Cool bro, glad you surfed with some dudes you want to be. Can you lose your hard-on so you can get back to teaching me how to use this database? Or forget about the database and at least tell me the necessary details of where the good surf breaks are on base instead of fantasizing out loud about your bromances.

MIFC LANT reserve duty meant driving down one weekend a month from DC to Virginia Beach

Fifty miles of Google's deepest red traffic hues? How am still seventy-five miles away from being stuck in the Norfolk tunnel?

The drive wasn't bad until summer, when vacation traffic between DC and Virginia Beach turned my normally three-hour trip into a six-to-eight hour, hot and humid nightmare. I was going nowhere, surrounded by thousands of eager family vacationers in minivans with excessive roof storage units.

The reservists at the MIFC LANT unit were fine. I worked with people who were intelligence professionals in their regular job and generally did well and took it easy. I was supposed to prove my proficiency at a few things so I could be qualified to do other things, but once I qualified to do other things, I would be doing those things on a night shift schedule. I was not excited about taking on night shifts for the weekend and then driving home to DC immediately after.

I dragged my heels on the qualifications at MIFC LANT and my Reserve Officer application was accepted. I would be attending the Coast Guard's Reserve Officer Candidate Indoctrination in two weeks.

Finally, one step closer to being able to do things how I think they should be done.

I escaped the night shift with no one caring about my concerns. I disliked that the other reservists were going to be put on that weekend night schedule and then go work their regular job Monday morning or have to take the day off from it. Most were already taking

Friday off so they could make the drive from however many hours away they lived from the unit. It seemed like a lot to ask of people whose weekend reserve duty tied together two work weeks into a 12-day work marathon.

Night shift also did weird things to my mind and body. While active duty in Key West, our teams had a nauseating back and forth from day to night shifts, mostly due to poor scheduling by supervision rather than mission needs or lack of resources.

Three nights working, one night off, then two day shifts, then a night shift again?

Once, I walked through the grocery store produce area near the store entry. It was cool and colorful with fruits and green veggies. The mist from the lettuce hit me as I reached over for a fresh stalk of celery. The spray gave me a full body chill. I looked at my watch and it read eight o'clock.

Eight? Eight. It's eight. Which eight? I panicked.

I didn't know if it was 8 a.m. or 8 p.m. I was in uniform. Was I *leaving* work or *on my way* to work? I had just walked into the store from my car, how did I not know which part of the day it was? I felt like I had woken up from a hard nap, experiencing that clueless fear caused by having no idea what time it was. It felt like a temporary frenzied panic that I had overslept. I wasn't arising from a nap, though; I was wide awake, attempting to restock on salad and ginger tea. I felt like I was a little crazy. Pulling out my phone, I confirmed it was eight in the morning, rubbed my temples to get it together, and returned to shopping.

I guess it's better to feel crazy than to fall asleep while driving.

Except for my own research on how to keep some kind of circadian rhythm during erratic schedules, I didn't receive a lot of guidance from anyone on what to consider in my routine, other than muscling through it. In addition to tricks and tips, mostly from those in the nursing field, I found there were plenty of articles for supervisors about how to create a good schedule for people. It just takes some reading and a few adjustments with your Excel sheet for someone to at least attempt to give slight regularity when possible.

Studying Homeland Security with a focus on Public Health made me keenly aware that first responders are needed in the best shape they can be in so they can do their job in emergency situations. Most of the support for them is enabled by organizational leaders and facilitated by supervisors. As much as I was happy to escape MIFC LANT's poor scheduling, I was also happy to be going into a designated leadership position by becoming an officer.

CHAPTER 21

SOUTHERN VIRGINIA
PART . . . XIV

By now, I knew to lower my expectations for Coast Guard training. Prior to officer candidate indoctrination, I mentally prepared to be cleaning sailing boats rather than setting sail.

"A LITTLE ANTHRAX NEVER hurt nobody," the unit chief made a farfetched joke about poisoning a colleague who was higher on the promotion list than one of our office mates.

"Um, Chief, actually, it did," an enlisted subordinate laughed and corrected him as two junior officers looked at each other wondering if they were obligated to address the anthrax statement.

The Reserve Officer Candidate Indoctrination was Officer Candidate School lite, designed for those who had already experienced military training. It was three weeks of training for enlisted personnel from other military services who wanted to join the Coast Guard officer ranks. It was also open to Coast Guard enlisted personnel who held a certain rank or an undergraduate degree. The training was one week of being treated like shit, another week of days overly packed with leadership courses and exercises, and the last week to take it down a notch and reflect on our leadership philosophies.

The first week's bullshit felt more like old-school hazing techniques. We had to *square* our meals, which involved not looking down at our plates, using our chosen utensils to pick up our food, raising it straight up from the plate to mouth level, then bringing the food into our mouths in a straight line. The upwards and then in motion had to be done at a ninety degree angle, making it like the corner of a square. All of this without looking down. It was tricky; if food fell off the utensil, you couldn't look down to pick it up, you had to search for it blindly or move on to another piece of food on the plate. I spent my meals staring at the Adam's apple of the person across from me as I ate.

This is really unappetizing.

One day the meal included peas. Davis, who was across from me, only had a fork. I decided to look down slightly to watch how he was going to achieve this feat of eating peas with a fork. Davis was a determined dude. He was a firefighter from North Carolina and former football player. Now, he was using his God-given talent to eat small round vegetables off a utensil not made for anything like that. I had so many questions for him. Why eat the peas? Why not go for something with bigger gains? Were peas his favorite vegetable? Did he think he needed more fiber? We weren't allowed to talk during the meals, so I stopped asking myself questions and began to play everything I was watching like a sporting event.

He's only got a fork, what is he going to do with that! I don't know if he can pull it off, but let's see!

He's got a single pea on board and one pea on deck. He's bringing it up, slowly, steadily. He's getting close to the top of that upward movement. Oh! The pea fell. That's gotta hurt. He's shaking his head. He knew he could have had that one.

Second chance. You don't always get second chances in this game, but here he goes. He's got three peas on that fork, must be feeling ambitious, and is making his move! He's made it past the upwards movement, they don't always make it that far. He's bringing it in. Oh and all three peas fell! I can't imagine what he's feeling right now!

It happened one more time before I burst out a snort of laughter. Then I tried to hide my laughter by looking down.

Oh shit. I looked down.

"*Walsh!* Did you just look *down?*" the instructor pretending to rage yelled, giddy that she got to mess with someone. "*Nose to the wall!*"

I got up, leaving my barely eaten meal behind to put my nose on the wall while the instructor moved around yelling at me. It lasted only about thirty seconds because she knew I still had to eat, "*Back to your table!*" I went back to my seat and looked at Davis.

"Worth it," I whispered, trying not to laugh again.

There was a lightness to the training, especially once the first week was over. It's like they wanted us to actually learn instead of fretting about trivial things. The training gave me a hierarchical boost of confidence because I now wore an insignia that meant I did not have to put up with asshole enlisted people in the same way I used to. I could also check in on others, with authority, to make sure none of what I experienced was happening to anyone else. Other than those perks though, I was at the bottom of the officer hierarchy.

We received our orders for our first assignment at the end of the course, "Fort Eustis? That sounds familiar," I said. We had our phones back on us, so I looked it up. The pin for Fort Eustis dropped about three miles from Yorktown, Virginia, where the intel training school was located. "I guess it will be a shorter drive than to Virginia Beach."

"Better get used to it, Ensign Walsh," the instructor, who turned into a peer now that training was over, came to provide words of wisdom. "There are fewer and fewer reserve billets as you move up the ranks, in about four years you'll probably be flying across the country for your drill weekend!"

I probably won't be.

"That sounds terrible. Thanks for your help, sir!" I turned around, shoved my paperwork back in its manila folder, grabbed my bags, and walked out. The training was solid; I was feeling good and I didn't want to hear any other Coast Guard Reserve truths.

Fort Eustis was named after Abraham Eustis, a military general who served in both Seminole wars in the 1800s. The wars included some of the fiercest battles of the US government against Native Americans. Eustis, in particular, was known for his skills in surveying and mapmaking. He created maps that allowed the military to move without getting stuck in the swampy, jungle areas of the South. He allowed for the blazing of trails, including the Trail of Tears, having commanded a base built to enable the violent forced removal of the Cherokee.

Recently, the Air Force had taken on half ownership of the base. Given the Air Force's more artful priorities, the facilities improved drastically. The on-base hotel was actually clean, the newly constructed buildings were built with materials other than heavy concrete, and the gym didn't smell like feet.

The Coast Guard Port Security Unit, however, was leasing property on base. The Coast Guard did not have ties to the Air Force or Army budgets. We were in a giant hangar that had been hastily divided into rooms as they were needed. In other words, there was no planning involved. The space was terrible for anything other than mustering 150 people in the same giant room for five minutes to close out every reserve weekend.

"Where did you say my locker was located?" I asked.

"Ma'am, the lockers are across the street and through the chain-linked fence in the weapons building, but not in the weapons section of the building, in the other door closer to boats. Here, I'll show you."

According to my orders, I was going to be the new *Shoreside* officer at the unit. Shoreside was the division of the unit made up of people who knew how to use guns and do things that were not on boats, like setting up entry control points, manning defensive fighting positions, and conducting patrols. Upon arrival, my assignment was changed to *administrative officer* under the logistics branch. I wasn't sure exactly what my job was, since there was already a logistics officer, but I accepted that it was at least a better fit. It worked out okay until a year later when that role was deleted from the organizational manual.

As a coveted administrative officer, I still had to go to the Port Security Basic Training, part of the Coast Guard's Specialized Mission Training Center on Camp Lejeune in North Carolina. It was a land-based training where we learned land navigation and patrols all while living in tents and doing other things not normally relevant to the Coast Guard.

In my civilian role, the other weeks and weekends of my life, I was about to leave my contracting job with the Department of Homeland Security and accept the role I was offered at the Department of State. When I reported to the Coast Guard unit, they asked if I could go to the two-week training the next week. Being essentially in between jobs, I said sure.

"The training course doesn't have enough participants. If you don't go, they will have to cancel the class."

"Sure thing!" I was fresh out of my officer leadership training. Besides being good timing for me, I was ready to serve and help out.

Because I was new to the unit, I had zero related qualifications. This meant that to attend the training, I required a waiver saying I wasn't yet trained in things I was supposed to train in before going to the training. That included waiving the rifle qualification. I had not shot any gun since Montauk and even then, I did not have consistent enough experience to want to keep up with the qualification, so it lapsed.

What if I'm in the Coast Guard personnel database as rifle qualified even though I can't remember the first thing about loading the gun! I have no idea what scenario would cause the Coast Guard to call me up for service requiring a rifle, but I'd rather not be on that list.

It turns out that I wasn't allowed to carry a real rifle at training, I could only carry around a stupid fake rifle that I thought I would never see again after bootcamp.

The training had good vibes—caring instructors and a good group of reservists attending from Port Security Units from around the country. The first day, we hiked as a group through sandy areas of Camp Lejeune to arrive at a large field surrounded by woods that would be our camp site for the next two weeks. I was an officer now, which meant I didn't have to do the manual labor of putting up the tents. I could finally take my big picture skills and help with planning the camp site layout, instead of pretending I knew how to stick the tent poles together in a way that would keep the canvases in place.

"Alright, what do we have to do with these?" I lifted a large plastic sheet that smelled like mildew.

"Miss Walsh, *we've* got this," a junior enlisted person assured me before I tangled myself in tent liners.

Not being involved in the manual details enabled me to do other officer things, like screw up land navigation. As part of the training, we were split into two teams that would navigate from one point to another using a compass and a map. The session was timed to encourage the teams to make decisions quickly and to make sure there was an end to it if either of the teams got really off track. We set off from our starting points in our Coast Guard specialized mission camouflage uniforms that were tan and green instead of the usual dark blue Coast Guard uniforms. The fabric was stiff and mine was incredibly bulky; I felt like a child in an older sibling's hand-me-down clothes that I still needed a few years to grow into. I managed to put on my body armor and throw the strap across my chest that carried my rifle. It was all a bit heavy. I was supposed to feel badass, but I was sure I looked ridiculous.

At least my sweat will be camouflaged.

The person leading my team in land navigation was an enlisted fellow, Peters. He had been at the unit for a while and knew how to do everything we were learning. Based on his guidance, the group would walk a certain direction a certain number of paces and then stop, check the map, and we would reevaluate. The first time we stopped, Peters said,

"Alright, we are going to go north now."

"North?" I objected while looking at my compass. "I have northwest."

Peters checked his work, tracing his finger on the map, then re-examined his compass. He looked me over for a split second, and nicely said, "Ma'am, your rifle is too close, the metal is pulling the compass off track." I was carrying my rifle on my side, instead of toward my back.

We started again, twenty paces north, then stopped to evaluate.

"Alright, now east," Peters declared, "anyone have anything different?" he asked, trying to include the team in the decision making.

I had a different answer on my compass, "Peters, I think we've got to go west," I said.

"Ma'am," Peters said softly so that the rest of the group wouldn't hear, "your rifle." He motioned to the strap.

Damn rifle.

I decided it was my turn to be passive and enjoy the experience. I was quiet until we came right next to a large swampy area. My boots started sticking to the smelly mud as we approached. We were walking through North Carolina's humid summer heat and now we hit the mud that its afternoon storms created. The land navigation course had us walking through the swamp to reach our destination.

"Continuing north," Peters said, and the group began to step toward the swamp.

"Wait," I stopped the group and slung my rifle to my back.

"Ma'am," Peters started, about to point to my rifle.

"Nope," I cut him off, "we are not walking through that swamp. We still have four more days of training. How many of you all brought along extra pairs of boots?"

No one raised their hand. I certainty hadn't.

"Peters," I took out the map, "I think the swamp will be more manageable over here, I pointed to a corner that had some lines showing it was higher ground, "how much time will that add?"

"Not long, maybe another ten minutes," he checked his watch, "yeah, we'll be fine."

We walked away from the mud pit and through a grassy area that sloped upwards. The end point was in sight from the top, but as we came down the hill toward our completion spot, we could see that the other group was reaching it first. We were still within the allotted time, but we had clearly lost the friendly competition aspect of the course.

"Well, we didn't win," one of our team members grumbled as we approached the group of dudes in their Oakleys and camo uniforms with knee high muddy water residue. I felt bad that we lost, almost wondering if we should have walked through the swamp.

Maybe I am not getting this leadership stuff right. Some of these guys look really bummed out for losing. Maybe I am lame and selfish and should have charged through the mud with them.

Peters jogged ahead toward the other team, "maybe we didn't win, but we're gonna be a lot more comfortable tomorrow!" he said as he slapped his whining team mate on the back. "And you all," he pointed to the other team, "ya better be in the other tent tonight cuz I am *not* dealing with your nasty-ass soggy gear."

Hell yeah.

What a difference that stupid gold bar on my collar made. I had no idea what I was doing, and I almost got us completely off track more than once. We didn't heroically storm through the water to reach our destination in record time, *but* I did my part to save us from wearing swampy boots the rest of the week.

CHAPTER 22

OFFICER DYNAMICS

When I was enlisted, I was always fucking up.
When I commissioned and became an officer, it suddenly
became way easier to fuck down.

NOW THAT I WAS an officer, enlisted dudes found me ten times more attractive than they did when I was at their level. These were the same types who would have only wanted to harass me when I was enlisted. I was the same person, the same looks, the same personality, but now that I had an officer bar on my collar, I was now the fantasy that some enlisted guys wanted to achieve. Lil Wayne's 2008 fantasy song, "Mrs. Officer," about hooking up a cop didn't help the narrative.

Despite this interesting and new dynamic, for me, dating within the unit was an easy and definite *no*. I would be working between Virginia and Guantanamo Bay for a while. I wasn't a huge fan of dating apps, but I had just been assigned a six-month deployment at the unit; give a single girl six months on a joint military base and she is going to find some entertainment. At first, the apps were a research tool that provided a feel for the area demographics. When I was living in DC, I got a few responses from guys I messaged, but in Southern Virginia, my response rate was near 100 percent.

Military towns might not be so bad after all.

I met a nice Army fellow, and we went on a date without talking about rank. He was tall, broad shouldered, and blond, with a dark blond mustache. He was friendly and warm—like a big gentle bear.

"Oh, you surf? That's awesome, I'm a diver," he said.

We bonded over a couple of dates; he was super sweet and enthusiastic.

"You paint! I know a super cool spot we can paint and drink wine. You bring the brushes, I'll bring the bottle." Another super cute date.

"Okay, meet me at my car at 4 p.m. today. I'll be parked at the Army dive locker. I have something in my trunk for you."

In the trunk? I hope it's not a puppy. I don't think it would be in the trunk if it was a puppy. What needs to be in a trunk? Is he going to kidnap me?

I drove to the parking lot and spotted him at his car, a black Mustang.

Dammit. He must be enlisted.

All his buddies were already in their cars, pulling out of the parking lot. Black and red Ford Mustangs and Chevy Chargers were the trademark cars of enlisted guys who returned from their first deployment and were able to pay cash for their vehicle of choice, within reason. Enlisted gals didn't seem to have that connection to those car types; my girlfriends in Key West mostly drove Toyota Corollas or Camrys. I didn't see any women pulling away from this lot so I couldn't validate my findings.

It was winter and the sun was starting to set. It gave an orange glow that radiated off the one-story brick building that was the dive locker he had spoken of. In front of it, his trunk was open, and he leaned on the car, giving me a big grin under his mustache.

"Check it out!" He was too excited to wait for me to get all the way to the car to look into in the trunk. He reached down and pulled out a black wetsuit, then put it back down in the trunk. He reached down again and this time came out with a pair of black surf booties.

"Oh my god! Wow, that's awesome, thank you." I reached the car and felt the wetsuit with one hand before giving him a hug. I pulled the wetsuit out to examine it. It was brand new with tags. The boots too. I didn't recognize the brand.

"It's the same stuff we use! I snagged you an extra," he said.

Wait. You're giving me Army dive gear?

I let that thought pass and gave him another hug, "You are so thoughtful. Wow." It wasn't even about the wetsuit or booties. I adored how excited he was to give these things to me. I couldn't express how cared for I felt, even if the gifts *may* have been stolen Army dive gear. He reminded me of a guy I dated in college who got me a burrito after every surf session. It wasn't until the fifth time that I realized he never paid for the burritos. He also made me an unknown accomplice in at least two dine and dashes.

"Let's get dinner!" The Army guy opened the passenger door for me to get in and closed it for me like a gentleman.

In the coming days, I found out that although my reserve position was no longer in our organizational manual, I would have to revoke my dating plans to actually go to Guantanamo to meet with the rest of the unit that was already down there. Such was life of being a woman on the move. I wish it was as sexy for a guy to wait for his woman to come back from deployment as it was for women waiting for their military hero man to return.

I said goodbye to this young, kind stud and prepared myself to put in the deployment work. I would *not* be dating in Guantanamo. Being a leader who was female, especially in the military, means leaving your sexuality at the door when working with these guys. Especially now that I was an officer, 90 percent of my peers were married anyway, and that is not worth anyone's time. I was going down there as a single working woman, a prior intelligence specialist with limited skills in boats and guns, at a unit that was entirely boats and guns. I was hoping for a little sunshine and pretend respect.

CHAPTER 23

DON'T GTMO BETTER
THAN THIS

*The therapist asked me if I thought I should go on anti-depressants.
I told her no, I just need more people to be on depressants.*

I THINK GUANTANAMO BAY prison is one of the biggest wastes of US taxpayer dollars and one of the Coast Guard's most demoralizing additional missions. Not only does the US pay thirteen million dollars per year, per prisoner, with the costs of court and prison being six billion dollars since 2002, but because there are high-value prisoners on the island, there are also tons of resources being spent to secure the area. The US Coast Guard patrols maritime areas around the prison around the clock. There are also Coast Guard- and Marine-led outposts where guns and people sit all day and all night ready to fire on the potentially IED-filled enemy ships. The potential attackers would likely be terrorists who want to blow up the US base *because* we keep prisoners there in the continuous spiral of never-ending trials that then cost more money and protection resources.

Deploying reservists to Guantanamo (GTMO) year-round has to be the Coast Guard's biggest financial burden, if they weren't likely receiving the funds from the bottomless piggybank that is the DoD. My paygrade wasn't high enough to be privy to this information. The deployment to GTMO is all the burden of being far from home for duty without the ego-boosting clout of saving people from roofs during hurricanes. It all makes any deployment there not only a waste of resources, but also pretty depressing.

No one I spoke to had a real answer to why the Coast Guard was assigned to Guantanamo Bay Naval Base, except the typical answer that they have always been there. Our patrols didn't offer any legal loopholes to the DoD by being a law enforcement entity, unlike in the Caribbean where having Coasties on board a Navy ship meant that Navy ship could legally involve itself with boarding suspicious vessels and inspecting them for anomalies, like having four metric tons of cocaine on board. Nope, the Coast Guard was under the same authorities as the Naval patrol boats.

On base, the Coast Guard had a few designated trailers and a boathouse—all arranged as if our stay would be temporary. It made no sense to me or any of my colleagues why the Coast Guard was in Guantanamo and this chapter exists because I have no explanation and I was part of a unit that had to go there.

When I received orders to report to my unit to begin deployment preparation for Guantanamo, I didn't know what terrorists were still locked up at GTMO. After all, it was 2017 and I thought that terrorist capture stuff happened in the early 2000s.

Did we not *execute the people who plotted 9/11? Would that be a war crime? Why are they still alive? Now I'm pissed at them for 9/11 and for making this deployment exist.*

Turns out there were still bad dudes at Guantanamo, some with fucked-up eyes and long beards. Their names and captures had become intelligence training case studies. I already hated Khalid Sheikh Mohammed and al-Baluchi, but now, it was more personal.

After the initial background research as to why the prison was still there, I continued to be annoyed about being called up on orders. I had just finished a long training course for my civilian position with the State Department when I received an email with the details of when I must report for duty to work for the Coast Guard full time at Fort Eustis and possibly Guantanamo. I called my Coast Guard supervisor.

"Am I really needed for this deployment? It starts less than two weeks after that long training for the federal job I just started."

"All personnel are going to be on orders. This is the first time the Coast Guard is deploying all of the Shoreside division to Guantanamo. All hands on deck! You'll be in Virginia for the majority of the time. This is a career building opportunity."

"I think my State Department job is where my career building opportunity lies, they just paid a lot of money to train me. Can I be on shorter orders and then jump on longer if it turns out you need my very unique administrative officer skills? What *is* my role now that the admin position doesn't exist in the org manual?"

"Walsh, I will see you January second."

Dismissed. I looked up what it would take to be a conscientious objector but didn't see any solid prospective paths to my own freedom.

How am I supposed to have a relationship if I am never if one spot?

There's not usually a great time in anyone's life to go on year-long orders; I was particularly peeved that this came at a time when I was just about to settle in my civilian job and new city of DC. I was looking forward to some normalcy for at least a year or two. If the deployment was for hurricane relief for a couple months or another noble cause, maybe I would have been more willing, but island prison camp did not get me excited about my service. I contacted a lawyer who tried to help, but there was no way out of this without a good steward in leadership to cut me a break.

I got a slight break. Another officer was an FBI agent and also requested some flexibility because he had just finished *his* training. The two of us would split the year with a six-month deployment for each us. That was as reasonable as leadership was going to get and seeing how they treated others, I considered myself lucky.

There was a health service (HS) technician at the unit, an HS1 who had been in the Coast Guard for eighteen years, so she only had two years until she qualified for retirement. HS1 was a nurse in her civilian job; she had two children and her husband was active-duty Coast Guard. She knew her family could not handle her being gone for a year, so she requested to be exempt from going to Guantanamo and offered to instead work from the base in Fort Eustis. She had submitted paperwork to transfer to a different reserve unit months ago, but the change in command at the unit disrupted the processing, which is a nice way of saying that the new command threw all old requests into the trash.

"Isn't there a system where we can find another HS for the deployment? I thought there were plenty of reservists who actually want to go." I flipped through HS1's deployment exemption request as I tried to talk out other options with my supervisor, who would make the call on the request.

"Yep! There is an online system. We already found one. She will take HS1's position when she resigns."

"She's resigning? But she has eighteen years in."

"The new technician, HS2, is going to report next week." She ignored my side of the conversation. "She's a recent college grad so she can handle the demands of being a reservist," the woman said to me, as if we were all martyrs for the Coast Guard.

"HS1 is a nurse," I countered, even though no one was listening. "We're going to replace her with a college grad? Couldn't we keep HS1 around on base to train the new HS to go to Guantanamo? Or is there a unit that needs an HS we could transfer HS1 to?"

None of the options I proposed that called out the false dichotomy of *go to GTMO or leave the reserves* were welcomed. HS1's request was firmly denied.

Do they not want HS1 to reach retirement? Is the Coast Guard trying to purge people from the reserves? What is their deal?

"Perhaps her last eighteen years of service didn't fully demonstrate her dedication," I said sarcastically to a colleague who also tried to keep HS1 onboard with the reserves.

I do not think that anyone was trying to be the exception to having to deploy, but maybe they were looking for a little flexibility considering there were reservists around the country who would gladly step in. Unit leadership did not seem to see reserve members as assets that the Coast Guard should try to retain.

We're hiring! #joinUSCGReserve, the Coast Guard Reserve Twitter account tweeted a few days after HS1 resigned, with a photo of their white patrol boat cruising through blue ocean waters. The contrast between what the unit did to HS1 and what the greater Coast Guard Reserves needed, more people with skills, was at best ironic. The reality was that the Coast Guard Reserves probably needed HS1 more than she needed them.

Why was this logistics officer on an ego trip allowed to run out a qualified person when the reserves at large needed qualified people?

I picked my battles and was not winning many. The new HS was great though, even if slightly inexperienced.

"No one should be sleeping with anyone in the Army," the new HS explained to a few of us once we were in Guantanamo. She provided a brief summary of important topics that came up during her daily health services meeting with all the military service health personnel on the Guantanamo Base. "The Army's STD rate right now is something like 25 percent. And those are people who are coming in for testing!" Without revealing personal information of those who got tested, she told everyone what they needed to know about which services to avoid, statistically speaking. In an uneventful place like Guantanamo, a little sexually transmitted disease gossip was all you could ask for.

The logistics officer who gave HS1 the boot, though, I could have done without her. She did her logistics work in her head and had difficulty organizing any documentation that could be passed down to someone else. She was the kind of person who felt powerful when she was the only person who knew certain information.

"Why can't she just give me the spreadsheet?" a fellow reserve officer vented to me after he walked out of a meeting. He was 6'4 and a physically built FBI agent in his civilian job. The logistics officer had stayed in the meeting room to schmooze the command, so he and others spoke freely in the hallway.

"You might steal her glory of presenting the number of boats in the water to the commander at the noon meeting," another lieutenant chimed in. "You know she looks forward to that all month, waiting to tell someone something she knows."

"Actually, there are three *boats in maintenance,"* the giant FBI agent put his hand on his hip obnoxiously, doing his best impression of how she had corrected him in front of the command. "Man, I thought we solved this information hoarding bullshit after 9/11."

It was all frustrating. Between being far from home, managing incompetence, and starting orders right after the New Year, morale was not great with anyone. However, fifteen days into the deployment, I checked my bank account and calmed down. I was making two times what I made as a civilian employee with half of it being an untaxed housing allowance. I was about to be mostly miserable living out of a hotel in Fort Eustis, Virginia and then heading to Guantanamo Bay, but I was seeing where the benefit would be.

I landed in Guantanamo after the rest of the unit had already been there a month. I flew in on what was a commercial plane, just operating from a military base. I was provided peanut snacks and everything. On this part of the deployment, I had two priorities: save money and make sure the enlisted folks weren't so overscheduled that they didn't have time to work out with me at the gym or snorkel at the beach before our night shifts.

What am I supposed to be doing here?

I filled my days with snorkeling, hiking, and long lunch breaks trying on military discounted Roxy bathing suits at the Exchange. It all seemed worthless.

How are people going to last a year here?

My job was sitting overnight in a radio room supervising the watch stander, who kept track of where our boats were by communicating with them over the radios. Most of the people I was supervising were equal or sometimes higher ranking than me in their civilian jobs. The unit was a mix of federal professionals, police officers, students, and IT personnel. None needed much supervision in their civilian job or their role on the radios.

"Walsh, what the heck are you doing?" the watch stander asked one night.

"I'm making flash cards," I shrugged. I had decided to spend my twelve-hour watches studying for the psychology graduate school test. "What if I never recover from being out of my job for so long?" I asked him.

"Give me those," he snatched the flash cards out of my hand and read one. "'A psychotherapist determines that a client's depressive symptoms may be the result of their interpretations of events in their life. Her theoretical orientation is most likely based on which of the following?' Walsh, you better learn all this quick—for yourself and the rest of us."

Making meaning out of Guantanamo was everyone's struggle. I was expected to blindly believe in the mission of the base and get others on board and connected to the Coast Guard's reason for being there. I could barely muster up the voice to say, "To defend freedom," in response to the gate guards saluting me and saying, "honor bound."

This reminder every time I cross onto base is not helping me figure out why I am here.

Everyone in the unit was beginning to try to find their own meaning to the deployment.

"KSM. His trial is delayed until next year." Some deployed members looked up information on the prisoners and began to follow the never-ending judicial proceedings to form a connection to where they were. Most people created a workout schedule and struggled through the long days of nothingness waiting to get to the gym and occasionally checking their bank accounts when they were feeling down.

Eventually, my six months on orders ended while others were going to carry on for another six.

I felt guilty leaving, but also deserving. The other officers had been off active duty for years and already created their careers and lives outside the Coast Guard. I was being pulled from one training to another, barely touching down in the city that was supposed to be my new home. I kept in touch with some of my colleagues in Guantanamo over text, but for most of them, it was easier to mentally stay in their routine and not be reminded of the world that kept going without them.

"7.2 million dollars," I texted, "I estimated the total amount of just our unit's paychecks per year in GTMO."

"Walsh, you're on the plane home and finally doing admin work!"

I never made it to the level of leadership where I could talk big budget stuff and question parts of the Coast Guard mission. Guantanamo's meaning for me was that I might not be able to handle the reserves much longer. I liked my position, I liked my peers, but the Coast Guard saying "semper paratus" (always prepared) meant being always prepared for bullshit too—and I was over it.

CHAPTER 24

WHO NEEDS THERAPY?
OH YEAH, ME

The therapist told me I had a "flat affect."
I was like, "Are you sure? I do squats at the gym every night."

THE DEPLOYMENT ENDED UP giving me what I needed: time in the sun, money in the bank, and a network of enlisted colleagues to help me fix my car issues. I showed up for the deployment with the side mirror duct taped to my car because I had sideswiped a trash can a few days earlier. By the end of my orders, thanks to guidance from the crew, I had a new mirror and a freshly painted car. Even with that kind of moral support, it was time to end my reserve duty.

The long drives took up both Fridays and Mondays of my weekend and I was missing out on key development opportunities with my civilian job. In the reserves, I was a quasi-administrative officer, and any replacement could learn the job in a few days. Unit members might miss my sparkling personality and semi-disgruntled intolerance of shitty leadership, but that was about it. Two FBI agents and I all resigned from the reserves the same year. To keep people with complimentary skills, the reserves would have to stop valuing unwavering dedication and start valuing the perspective and experience that dedicated professionals bring to the organization.

Following my service, the Department of Veterans Affairs (VA) determined that I needed a little bit of therapy. After two years of being processed for treatment, I finally received a few therapy sessions paid for by the VA.

The therapist had an in-home private practice and when I arrived at the address, I was pleased to see I was at a large house just outside of DC in the ritzy area of Bethesda, Maryland.

Wow, she must be doing well in her private practice! I bet the inside is furnished entirely in Restoration Hardware pieces. She has to be doing these VA appointments like some kind of pro bono work.

The office would *obviously* be located in one of the wings of the house, where we'd have some privacy from her East Coast kids rocking polo shirts with popped collars and dapper husband ready to pour his wife a glass of rosé before dinner.

It was around seven o'clock when I arrived that evening. I imagined the husband and children were likely about to come home from lacrosse practice. I looked forward to comparing notes with this woman on the Hamptons and bonding by scoffing at anything less than tasteful. After months of VA paperwork, I was excited to finally speak to an obviously successful and professional female psychologist.

I walked into a house, as instructed by a sign on the door, and a bell on the door handle jingled.

Okay. Interesting. It smells like a hamster's cage in here. Those dirty T-shirts hanging on the banister look like they've been there for a while. I guess I will keep my jacket on.

The bell was to notify the therapist from her couch that a patient had arrived. Three out of a total of fourteen obese cats greeted me and guided me into the living room. As I walked in, I saw that the rest of the cats were also obese and wandered around eating from various large, overflowing food bowls scattered around the living room throughout the session.

"Hello, Caroline." She greeted me from her spot on the couch that I guessed she hadn't moved from for most of the day—possibly yesterday too if she had slept there.

A 1970s food tray served as her desk; it had a cup of coffee from the morning on top, amazingly not yet knocked over by the cats.

The therapist was calm and down to earth but given her zoo-like environment and sedentary state, did not seem very healthy herself. She had thinning, wispy, light brown hair, big, thick, round 80s-style glasses with clear rims and wore something between a mumu and a nightgown.

She attempted to bond with me over living in California. "I tried to surf a few times, I see why you enjoy it," she said as I tried to, but could not imagine her trying to surf. Her ocean stories were well-intended, but over the next few sessions, she told me the same story, not realizing she had already told me these stories.

Maybe the wobbly food tray desk was preventing her from taking clear notes.

I wasn't sure why she was telling me stories, since it was *my* one-hour therapy session. I figured I was the one who was supposed to talk, but it was early in the therapist/patient relationship, so I let her take the lead. After all, she was the licensed psychologist, recommended by the VA, certified by the American Society of Clinical Hypnosis, and *a skilled animal communicator for all species*, according to the brochure I found in the foyer.

"So, what kind of therapy would you say you practice?" I asked in our first session.

"Holistic. I once had a patient who complained of migraines. PB2 healed those migraines in just a few sessions. PB2 would curl up around her neck and then walk around her head."

"PB2 is the cat?"

"Yes, this one," she pointed to one of the many obese gray cats, "PB2 is one of the most intuitive. Oh look! Tatiana is coming up to you, I think I know what that means about your energy, let's see if she hops on your lap."

Tatiana was about to hop on my lap, but PB2 launched to chase her away.

"Oh that PB2! He is the leader. Tatiana is just a yearling. One of four yearlings. PB2 picks on all them, but it's okay because PB1 can handle PB2 and will come protect the yearlings. Or sometimes I have to swat PB2 away."

After the end of session three, I thought maybe we were almost getting somewhere; I had at least accepted that the hamster cage smell lessened in my nostrils after fifteen minutes.

"Some of my clients like to rub a little essential oil under their nose for the session. You are welcome to do so if you are bothered by the . . ." she stopped before she had to say "smell" and offered me the vile of eucalyptus oil.

"I'm okay," I said, processing that she was aware that her home smelled and not yet ready to take the oil because that would let her know that I knew of the smell, even though she had already known and knew that I knew.

I was ready for session four, but she had to cancel because she had the flu. We rescheduled for the next week, but she canceled again, this time in her voicemail I could hear the beeping of hospital monitors in the background. It must be a serious flu. Listening to the voicemail, I became worried about her cats. I knew they had enough food for about a month, but what about the pack dynamics.

What are the yearlings going to do if PB1 can't stick up for all of them against pack leader, PB2, for all this time? Plus! Muffins was starting to challenge PB2 for leadership and her brother might be the force to make that change happen. Plus! Who was going to clean the litter boxes?

The therapist didn't pick up any calls and soon her voicemail was full. A few weeks later, her daughter left me a message saying her mother had closed her practice. I searched the Bethesda obituaries for a while and didn't see her name.

I was eventually assigned a new therapist, but it was just not the same. I had hoped I could at least turn the cat therapist experience into part of my standup comedy routine, but I was at a loss for identifying the punchline. I also didn't mind the therapist that much; I am not completely opposed to having some animals around as a distraction from my problems. Besides, maybe by session ten, her cats would have cured my ailments like they did that poor woman's migraine. I will never know. *This story has zero exaggerations and I wish I had recorded the dialogue for even more accuracy.*

CHAPTER 25

SKIP TO THE INTERNATIONAL SPY STUFF ALREADY

I don't know how people write entire books about their job at the CIA. At the end of each day, with each departure from an internal office space to the outside world, what we were allowed to discuss diminished until it was nothing but office gossip. I was working in the compartments my therapists tried to have me break down.

"THAT'S DEFINITELY THEIR COMPOUND, what are we supposed to do about it?"

"What if we just fuck with them?"

"Yes! Can we drop anti-drug pamphlets to let them know we know what they are up to? I think I still have an old D.A.R.E. T-shirt."

"Why not drop something more impactful?"

"This isn't Pakistan. All we are probably authorized to drop here are glitter bombs."

"You know how hard it is to clean up glitter? That might be hilarious and amazing. Can you imagine the analyst translating their conversations afterward? What is *glitter* in Spanish anyway?"

"Glitter? What if we dropped the *Billy Madison* version of a bag of shit on fire?"

"Yes! Shit bombs!"

"Okay, okay," the manager spoke up, "I'm not sure if the lawyers will approve the fire power portion of something we're calling a shit *bomb* . . . what about balloons? If you really think this might lead us to something, put together talking points on what shit balloons would accomplish."

In the Coast Guard, when I wanted my idea to be heard, I had to repeat it five times at various meetings and in hallway discussions before a higher-ranking person would take my idea and present it as his own. I had ventured from not being heard in the Coast Guard, to then becoming a decently respected voice at the State Department, to now having to watch what I said in every offhand comment at the CIA because my colleagues of all ranks actually listened and were generally open to fresh ideas.

The evolution of glitter bombs into shit balloons at the CIA was immediately welcomed as part of the brainstorming process. Their brainstorming rules meant that nothing could be turned down in the initial phase of exploring options. Although these ideas did not go straight to the lawyers for approval, I *was* allowed to mention the idea during a discussion with the lawyers about alternative options.

"I'm going to need more about how shit balloons will lead us toward our strategy end goal before I can approve this." The lawyers were a fine use of checks and balances on creativity within the Agency.

Agency brainstorming was sometimes creatively destructive and without proper moral courage, could get less-than ideal, sometimes other-than humane results. In recent history there were issues with the CIA's enhanced interrogation techniques, which included physically coercive interventions such as waterboarding, sleep deprivation, facial slapping, forced standing, etc. These techniques were at first deemed helpful in producing foreign intelligence by the CIA, but then not an effective manner of obtaining intelligence by the Senate. The FBI stated that building rapport is generally accepted as the most key component of a successful interrogation, according to their High Value Detainee Interrogation Group document, *Interrogation Best Practices*, which is available online.

I spent a few days in a training course and had the privilege of hearing from a CIA targeter explain the work she did to track one of Al-Qaeda's top operatives, which resulted in that terrorist's detention at Guantanamo Bay. At the end, she said to the class, "and the jury is still out on whether we would have gotten the information we needed without the enhanced interrogations."

The students all looked at each other, wondering if she was allowed to close with that statement. As far as we were told in previous training courses, the jury was *in* that the Agency wasn't endorsing those techniques anymore.

I wondered whether the targeter had to put on this presentation like some sort of community service for her involvement in the Guantanamo/black sites ordeal. Her closing argument being the only chance to express how she truly felt. She seemed to relive her experience of tracking these bad guys to their end through her presentation. I wondered if this assignment was really in her best interest. She was in her forties, not a dinosaur with nothing left to give by any means. However, if it was fifteen years after this bad guy's detainment and she still had not decompressed from tracking and capturing one of the world's top terrorists. I don't know if a few extra weeks on vacation drinking margaritas and getting some sunshine were going to help.

Guantanamo and related operations were like the CIA's never healing wound. I stopped wearing the GTMO T-shirt from my Coast Guard deployment to the CIA gym because I think I was triggering officers with related experiences when they happened to glance at my shirt through the mirror.

One time a branch chief had nicely asked, "Oh you did a long deployment with your reserve unit, where was it to?"

"Guantanamo," I replied. His face contorted like he was having a flashback and simultaneously thinking of how to get out of this conversation.

"I know that place," he said, "not good times. I leave that one where it is."

Less tension and more creativity came when our office opened a remote branch in a tropical area. Despite the tropical surroundings, the office was windowless and overly air conditioned. It was like working in a giant freezer. We knew that outside a few layers of walls, the waves lapped at the beach and the temperature was warm and soothing. Without windows though, the teal blue water landscapes weren't visible unless we went through three badge entry/exit doors to get past the security desk to walk outside to thaw. My colleagues and I could not find any fleece blankets for sale at the local discount stores specializing in bikinis, sunscreen, and *I'm with Stupid* T-shirts. Warm and drunk vibes only.

To feel more connected to our tropical surroundings, when the boss was out sick, we brainstormed a name for our team.

"Tropical heroes?"

"Tactical palm trees?"

"Tiki hut hunters?"

"I know! *Tactical Tiki Hut!*" The name stuck.

After work, we immediately went to the dollar store and bought every tiki hut decoration that store had to offer. From banners to sparkling palm tree pop-ups, we spent approximately $30 (of our personal money) on morale-improving decor. We would never have ocean views, but the next day we had a blowup plastic monkey, named Gary, who stood watch for us. His only security failure was after hours when his monkey arm slipped off the door handle and caused the building security alarm to activate.

"I got a call from the security desk last night," our manager said.

"Oh shit! I thought we locked up. Did I forget to spin the lock?" my colleague responded.

"Nope, just uh, make sure that monkey stays in one spot, okay?"

"Fucking, Gary! Sorry boss."

We decorated just in time for a stream of congressional visits that month. Those visits are a chance for the offices to informally tell congress about our achievements so they continue to fund our programs. My peers and I were afraid that after all our hard work finally getting plastic flamingo cutouts to stick to the wall above the air conditioner, we would be stuck removing the decor, then redecorating after the visits, if at all. The boss stayed late to prepare for the visits.

"Do you, uh, need anything from us?" we asked before leaving.

"No, enjoy the evening," he said. The edge of his desk was lined with flowing green grass skirt material.

"I hope he doesn't take it all down himself," I said to my colleague as we walked through the various security turnstiles.

"Shit, we should have offered."

We arrived early the next morning, in our more formal attire, which was usual for these types of visits. We did our opening procedure, turning off the alarms, spinning open the lock, and slowly opening the door to the office.

"Oh my god. He didn't change a thing."

Even Gary was allowed to stay up to meet Congress, despite his past antics. I am sure they were impressed.

What is that girl doing?

She had just flipped an aggressive u-turn and her trailing surveillance team tried to adapt without making aggressive moves that would draw attention to themselves.

We were three weeks into a six-month training, and I had crossed into Laura's surveillance bubble of five cars that would rotate in following her throughout her route. Her job was to continue on her route and try to identify the trailing cars over normal traffic. I was doing the same. Laura was a typical-looking woman in her late twenties who could have blended in on any college campus with her pothead-like, easy-going demeanor. In class, she was often doodling on her notes and in her own world. Nothing seemed to bother her.

Dammit.

Seeing that our routes crossed paths meant I now had to distinguish between her surveillance and mine. I peered into my rearview mirror, *XV . . .* I couldn't get the whole plate before the light turned green. I looked ahead and saw her car screech back north from the left-hand turn lane, making a U-turn under a clearly marked *no U-turn* sign. Laura looked calm as always, but her moves were definitely not calm. I peered out my driver-side window to watch a number of average model cars try to catch up with her move. They clearly were not expecting anything so abrupt.

I guess those confused cars aren't part of my *surveillance.*

I refocused and continued on my route. Whatever Laura was doing was not part of the training. The surveillance detection runs were supposed to be a series of stops in which you determined whether you had surveillance and if you did, you tried to identify cars and drivers. There were to be no CIA movie chase scenes of losing your tail because that was not a realistic representation of operations and would definitely cause you problems when driving around overseas.

I had my meeting with the role player, who was a gluttonous old man pretending to be someone from whom I would elicit information over lunch and then plan a follow-on meeting. We met at a very inauthentic Mexican restaurant and he ordered fried cheese balls to start. He played the game slowly, giving me time to test out what we had learned. He also seemed to enjoy his position of power, where I was the student and person in the meeting who would have to make adjustments to his preferences.

"You don't want any of these cheese balls? They are my favorite! Please have some," he said.

Ugh I am supposed to be bonding with him . . . "you, me, same, same," as the instructors advised.

"Sure thing! They are my favorite too!" I said and stabbed a fried sphere with my fork. I kept talking, hoping he would not notice the untouched cheese ball on my plate.

"You haven't tried it yet!" he interrupted himself, after he had stuffed his mouth with five of them.

"Oh right! Sorry, your story is just *so* interesting," I grabbed a knife to cut the cheese ball in half and ate part of it.

He's definitely going to notice if I don't eat the whole thing.

I put the other half in my mouth, "so good!" I said and kept on with the conversation.

"You must have another!" he interrupted again.

He is completely enjoying this.

I ate three more cheese balls so he would give me the information I needed and left the meeting to go back and write up what I had.

As I was walking up to my room in a barracks-like structure, I saw Laura walking out one of the doors with all her things. She was too far away to get her attention and I was pressed for time in finishing my tasks related to the meeting. She didn't look upset. She looked like normal Laura with her head in the clouds. When I finished my write ups, I walked over to the dining hall to grab dinner.

"Did you hear what happened to Laura?" Christopher always knew what was going on with the everyone in the training group.

"No! Tell me! I saw her mess up her detection run *on purpose!*" I said, proud I could contribute to what is normally Christopher's all-knowing domain of gossip.

"She just decided she didn't want to do the training anymore!" Christopher laughed, "in the middle of the exercise." He shrugged. "So, she turned around, taking her surveillance all the way to the administrative building, checked out with them, and went home. I knew she was out there, but I did not see *that* coming." He paused, then continued, "I'm going to miss watching her color in shadows in all those clouds she draws on our handouts during class," he said, reminiscing momentarily. "Okay, now tell me about your meeting."

"Christopher! He made me eat *fried cheese balls!*"

"No! I really hope I don't get him next. I'm lactose intolerant!" he said with a dreadful look on his face. "No, actually, I'm not, but I would definitely say that," Christopher winked.

We laughed off the stress of the training and objectified hot guys who walked past our table, trying to figure out which team they played on.

"What about him?" I asked Christopher and motioned toward one of the former military guys.

"For me?" he asked.

"No! For me." I said.

"I really think he's for me. I *swear* I saw him at Number Nine," Christopher said, referring to his neighborhood gay bar.

"Christopher, this is not fair, your team is taking all the talent."

We reached our usual draw when it came to men and worked through the exhausting training. Laura, the U-turn subject matter expert, also continued at the CIA, but found an analyst role that was more suited to her style and did not require operational training. She likely continues to roam the CIA halls, partially in her own world, but clearly aware of herself and what she is willing or not willing to do.

CHAPTER 26

SPY STORIES

"We're not supposed to hack the NSA."

"I'm not hacking the NSA, I'm merely querying their databases."

MOST OF MY TARGETING work could be summarized in two movie quotes, "Finkle is Einhorn. Einhorn is Finkle!" The voice of identity discovery from *Ace Ventura: Pet Detective* often played through my mind when figuring out a bad guy's alias and finally putting together who was who in a network. On the slower days, I would replay the sad excuse for intel from the janitor in *Billy Madison*, "Billy likes to drink soda. Miss Lippy's car . . . is green." After looking to see if a dull intel report might be relevant, I would move on and catch up on the next document. Boring days or exciting, it all led to interesting travel opportunities.

So there I was in a country known for its drug trafficking problems and working with a bunch of dudes again. I walked down the rickety steps off the small plane into a hot and dusty environment.

This is better than the polluted air we had been breathing in the capital city. Plus, we survived that bumpy local airline flight.

I continued down the steps of the plane and went to meet the driver out front. We drove about forty-five minutes to another location where we would be working with our Latin American partners. I exited the car and was greeted outside by about five of them, all men, of course. I thought the Coast Guard would be the end of those extreme men-to-women ratios, but now I was in Latin America, expecting serious machismo culture to make things even more difficult. We started on our work for the day and most of the guys were respectful enough.

Our partners used a casual lunch to slow down and chat, which helped me take the edge off. They showed me photos of their families and the hikes with waterfalls they had done over the weekend. Family guys, it seemed. They were trying to help me feel comfortable with them, except for one who had been eying me all morning.

"Parece como mi hija," he finally said. "You look like my daughter."

Okay, sure, nice excuse, you are only saying that because I caught you staring at me.

He took out his phone, scrolled down a few photos and turned it for me to see the screen.

Oh god, what is he going to show me.

I leaned in slightly, and squinted to see the woman in the photo, "oh wow, si es mi gemela!" I was shocked. The woman looked like my twin; a Hispanic version of me.

The case officer I was working with on this assignment had much worse Spanish skills than I did, which made me embarrassed for him. He was a guy about fifty-something years old. Over the years he had probably put on some weight and lost some hair, but still saw himself as a varsity football ladies' man. He had recently transferred to the Latin America account after working years in counterterrorism. I felt for him in trying to figure out this new fit but can't say I enjoyed his presence.

"I'm going to hit the gym," he said one afternoon as he strolled into the office in his college T-shirt that he had obviously cut the sleeves off himself. It was gray and red and had stains like he had saved it from his previous frat party days. Besides telling me he was going to the gym, this case officer's favorite pastime seemed to be talking shit about this country in English during our taxi rides, as if no one in this country possibly spoke English or could put together *piece of shit*, *dirty*, and the name of the country.

He was not just annoying, I could roll my eyes at that, but he started to be more inappropriate than any of these Latin American guys who suffered the stereotype of being the ones to discount and disrespect women.

"Yeah, she's my work wife," he joked with one of the partners.

"Como?" the partner did not understand.

"Work wife. Mi e-spos-o de trabajo," he said in bad Spanish.

"Ah, nunca usamos esta frase." They had never used that phrase, the partner stated and changed the topic.

Later, I was checking into a hotel with the case officer when the front desk asked, "one room or two?"

"Well, I don't know," he looked at me and gave what he thought was a playful nudge with a double eyebrow raise.

"Dos, gracias." I didn't acknowledge the playful elbowing, I just tried to close the transaction as quickly as possible so I could go to my own room to watch E! News en Espanol and go to bed. Traveling was exhausting and this guy was draining. Only a few more days and I could leave. I was grateful my manager shut down his request for five weeks of assistance from me. I'm guessing he thought that timeline would get us down to one bedroom.

At the beginning of it all, I arrived at the CIA by way of a failed FBI interview.

"I see a problem here; when did this happen?" the FBI pre-polygraph interviewer asked about an incident from my youth. I sat in a dark office with gray walls and no windows. A giant black desk sat in between me and this man. He was in a cushy desk chair with wheels, and I sat in a folding metal chair. His dress shirt was overly starched and buttoned to the top collar, practically reaching his law enforcement-style, blond-with-hints-of-gray mustache.

"It was a long time ago and only once," I replied. I was doing my best at being open and honest, but in the room with only the desk lamp lights shining on me, I was starting to feel like a criminal being grilled by an asshole cop.

"What was the exact date of this activity again?" he asked, as if I really knew the exact month, date, and year of a night that I did something that definitely did not belong in my life, but I repeated the estimate.

The interview stopped, "Alright Ms. Walsh, we are going to have to end this interview," he said with no further explanation and walked me out.

Okay?

I did not want to press him, even though I was a grown adult applying to jobs where I would have a lot of responsibility. He had not made it seem like I was in a place where I got to ask any questions. I was used to that dynamic from the military hierarchy, so I walked to my car, went home, and waited. I received a phone call a few days later,

"Yes, Ms. Walsh, there's a bit of a problem with your interview," a woman said over the phone. "Yes, you can't have exposure to that within ten years of applying. FBI policy. Let's see, it was nine years ago, you'll be able to reapply in about five months. Have a nice day."

Reapply? I thought I would have a job within five months!

I had no idea how something like that, an incident I had almost forgotten about, could come back and burn me the way it did. I was embarrassed, especially since now I had to explain what happened to the mentor who worked at the FBI and guided me to the position that would have been the best fit. I told her what happened with about zero confidence in myself, but she was kind and encouraging.

"Oh, too bad it hadn't happened a few months earlier, you'd be right on time!" she said. "Yes, unfortunately, they are very strict about their drug policies."

Was she hinting I should have known their policy and fudged the date? Too late now.

When it came time for my interview with the CIA, I was a mix of nervous and apathetic. I had done well in the job interviews, tests, and writings that were required in the process, but I knew that none of that mattered if the organization's regulations were going to burn me again. I was open and honest in my interview before the polygraph, again listing my regrettable antics to be judged by people who held the green light or red light to my future career. I sat across from the psychologist interviewer. He was in a nice bright office with light wood decor, pleasant cream-colored walls, and family photos displayed around. It smelled like vanilla.

"It doesn't seem like you liked drugs very much," the CIA psychologist said. He had wispy gray hair and wore a festive holiday bowtie as he flipped through my folder and summarized my youthful antics.

"No, I didn't," I replied.

"Good luck with the rest of the process. I'm sure you'll get through just fine," he reached across to shake my hand, then walked me out of his office, smiled, and waved. I walked through the lobby with its teal and magenta modern chairs and big glass windows. Before pushing through the revolving doors to the cold winter sun, I stopped to sit on the bright blue chair. With my jacket on my lap; I looked up through the windows at the cloudless sky with the winter sun shining down. I put my hand on my chest and let out a sigh of relief.

I just might get this.

The CIA had it right based on what they do and who they need. If you are going to ask people to cross international borders using alias documents, you might not want it to be the first time they've done something illegal. I love my FBI partners, but as an organization, if you want to stay ahead of criminals, you might not want to eliminate people who have lived a little.

I was halfway through the career analyst training program when we watched a video in class that referred to analysts as the *tip of the spear*. The video ended and the lights came on. "Alright, take a quick break," the instructor told us. I walked out the doors with a friend toward the coffee spot where we liked to chat and gossip.

"Jerry," I said, "if I hear anyone else reference the *tip of the spear* like that, I'm going to walk out."

"What? What's wrong with saying tip of the spear?" he egged me on.

"Seriously? I thought it was just military that overused that phrase, now CIA too? It's like leaders like to tell their people they are the tip of the spear when they want to convince someone that their job is important. At the last unit I was at, a commander went on being encouraging, claiming the operations specialists he was talking to, who communicate with the planes over the radio, was the tip of the spear. Wouldn't the person flying the plane be the tip of the spear? Or the people on the boats doing the boardings? I get it, the operation specialist is important, but why do you have to tell him that to make him think his job is worthwhile?" I ranted.

"I see," Jerry let me continue.

"Now everyone and their mother has become the tip of the spear," my voice got louder as I thought more about the times I had heard this phrase used incorrectly. "An analyst is the exact *opposite*. The tip of the spear is someone who is knocking down doors, or shooting dudes from helicopters. Tell me what makes an analyst, who is writing reports and briefing, the tip of the spear! They are like the *opposite* end of the spear, an analyst is the what—the feather? What is at the other end of the spear?"

"I mean, a feather is at the other end of an arrow," Jerry offered.

"Okay, the feather, we, as analysts, aren't even the feather, we are like the bow of the bow and arrow, guiding the spear . . . arrow . . . whatever . . . guiding it to go where it is supposed to go. People need to stop using that phrase with everyone. It is worse than just telling everyone they are special."

"Point taken," Jerry sipped his coffee. "Caroline, I promise I will never use that phrase."

"Thank you," I sighed and ordered a decaf. Time to step off the soap box.

Two days later, a guest speaker came into the class. The lights dimmed and her PowerPoint lit up. A spear.

"TOTS," Jerry whispered loudly. "TOTS."

I turned around to look at him, "What are you saying?" I whispered back, but the presentation had already started.

Once it closed and the speaker left, Jerry came up to my desk, "TOTS! I can't believe she talked about TOTS! I was dying! You must be livid."

"Are you calling me TOTS?" I asked.

"Yeah! You like it? Your new nickname. TOTS—Tip Of The Spear. Everyone at that end of the spear deserves a nickname, you know that! It's perfect, it's like call signs, which everyone *also* overuses! The only people who need call signs are pilots, yet everyone has a call sign now! So, this is yours."

And so, TOTS became my call sign . . . between me and Jerry and a few other people in class who remembered the nickname only when Jerry yelled "TOTS" over the classroom to get my attention. Thankfully, it was not too sticky of a name. We mostly got weird looks of concern that he was harassing me when anyone outside the training overheard him calling me TOTS.

"Why is that place your top choice?" I asked.

"Well, I did some research," he explained, "at first I was torn between a few *very* appealing options. They all had beaches, night life, and great weather. However, after careful counting, what you would call *analysis,* I determined I would have the most days off if I was there."

"I don't understand. Why would you have more days there?"

"Because if I go there, I get the US holidays off and their holidays too—and they have the most holidays I've ever heard of! So obviously it is my top choice!" My colleague was a dedicated worker, but clearly was choosing his assignments wisely.

The CIA brought together people with a unique mix of intelligence and street smarts. Intelligence was emphasized, especially in the Directorate of Analysis, but often the underlying sentiment that set the Agency apart from other government organizations was the ability to adapt and make interesting decisions for themselves and for the mission.

Working in counternarcotics, I collaborated with organizations like the Navy and Drug Enforcement Agency. Not only were our cultures different, but our motivations made our focuses different.

"Why is DEA looking through all our posts?" a colleague asked while sitting at her computer. She was looking at the metadata that showed who viewed what we had written. Our desks faced opposite directions and we talked to each other without turning around. We were working with a few agencies on a counter drug trafficking project. We posted our updates in a joint database.

"That is weird."

"Wait, not all of them. They are only looking at the ones with geographical coordinates."

A button clicked on the door, it unlocked, and our manager walked into the room. He was an easy going, mid-thirties, guy and usually had a mix enthusiasm for the job with awareness of what the real priorities are in life. He cared a lot about the mission but had seen a lot of the CIA and was wise enough to know which battles were worth fighting.

"What's the latest?" he asked.

"DEA is being weird. They hardly talk to us and never responded to my email from yesterday yet seem to be sifting through our locational information."

"Typical DEA," he rolled his eyes. "They are probably trying to figure out the source of our information so they can use it, post before we post, and claim credit when there's a drug bust."

"Why do they care so much about credit?" my colleague asked hastily. DEA's lack of responses to her inquires had become personal. "Going through our information seems like a waste of time. We already have the source that enables drug busts! Why would they want to know it so badly? Why would they dedicate their own manpower to trolling our contributions? Don't they have other things they should be analyzing?"

"Well, you have to understand," the manager said, "their funding is pretty much linked directly to the amount of cocaine they bust. Kilograms equal dollars, not only to the drug trafficking organizations, but to the DEA themselves. They have a very narrow mission and very narrow ways to measure success."

It was hard to understand their organization's cultural desire for the glory and the headlines when our own organization was motivated to keep most successes inside our own walls and sometimes only within our office.

"Maybe if they dedicated their time to finding those kilos instead of looking our shit up like they are some Russian spy who infiltrated the National Rifle Association and is now trying to find Republican senators to give them information . . . they would keep their stupid funding," she tried to make a comparison to recent frustrating headlines.

"Concur," the manager said, obviously having dealt with the DEA's antics before and not wanting to get into it. "What are our happy-hour plans?" he asked to close the conversation before anyone got too frustrated.

CIA and DEA coordination was a culture clash in most environments.

"*Samson!*" another counternarcotics CIA manager leaned forward over the shuttle seat to quote his favorite stoner movie, *Half Baked,* in my ear. Our team was on our way to visit a DEA lab out in rural Virginia to go over the DEA's latest analysis. This manager was a smart, confident, shorter man who once told us he liked having a tall girlfriend because it, "made him feel rich." His general positive spin and playfulness made for a good work environment.

"Littering and . . . littering and . . ." We were inside the lab and a DEA analyst just passed around a giant vacuum-sealed bag of sticky marijuana flowers. It was the size of a small pillow and heavily marked with tracking information. Marijuana was a tricky topic because it wasn't a particularly dangerous substance but had potentially significant financials. Regardless, it was taking *someone* down memory lane, ". . . smoking the reefer," my manager whispered another of his favorite quotes a little too loud as he held the bag up to eye level to check out its quality. The DEA analyst waiting on the side of the room for his turn to brief heard the quotes and gave my manager a furrowed-brow look of strong disapproval. Our office could collaborate enough to get DEA's input on detailed lab trends, but chances of getting along with them were slim.

I served in a variety of places during my time as a targeting analyst at the Agency. Focuses included, counternarcotics, counterterrorism, holding China at bay the best we can, and our office of advanced analytics. Each office tended to take on the culture of the topic. Their differences were the clearest in each office's email around the holidays:

"Our Christmas celebration will be from *exactly* 12:15 p.m. to 1:15 p.m. Please be there *on time*. Here is a list of what each person needs to bring in order to enjoy the festive *hour*," read a direct and organized email from the China department leadership.

"Marg machine is on! It's Friday, so that means *twenty-five days* until the holidays! Come by the manager's office aisle for some music and margaritas to end the week," the counternarcotics office with the Latin America focus was looking for any reason to start things up on Friday after 11 a.m.

"Please give yourself a break *before* the holidays. Take a walk. Try a thirty-minute meditation. You'll feel better and be ready for work afterward!" read the counter terrorism leadership email, almost acknowledging that a terrorist cell was likely prepping for a holiday attack that would interrupt each employee's time at home.

"Hey everyone! Come to the holiday party and remember to *socialize*. We still have drinks left over from the last get together. Be sure to come to this one! At least stop in and say hi! Work/life balance is important!" The office of advanced analytics tried so hard to get their introverted, mathematic minds to awkwardly come together to talk about things in life other than regression analysis.

Each year during the holiday season, there was a lot of down time in the Latin American side of the counternarcotics office. Drug trafficking seemed to be at its slowest from Christmas until mid-February.

Are the drug traffickers on a break or are the government agencies who report on drug movements taking their vacation time now?

Either way, it seemed like a one-to-two-month truce that allowed me time every year around January for personal travel. The CIA made it hard not to see other countries through the lens of corruption and political instability, but it never hurt to have a little extra foreign language training to get me around to the solid global surf spots.

CHAPTER 27

SHIT AND BOOBIES

My Peruvian friend thought we should move to Peru because of how badly US politics have divided the country in recent years. That's where we are at. People living in a near narco-state like Peru are concerned about our wellbeing. Then again, maybe it is time to try living at the other end of the cocaine supply chain.

"FISHERMAN HUNDREDS OF YEARS ago saw this island glistening with streaks of silver in the sun and named it, *Isla de La Plata*, Island of Silver," our tour guide explained. It was not until they landed on this little island that they would find out that the precious shining silver streaks were not silver, but epic collections of white bird shit.

The poor man's Galapagos was our fix for wanting to keep our trip simple while also appeasing those pesky post-vacation questions, "Oh, you went to Ecuador, did you see the Galapagos?" With this trip, we could answer that we most certainly did. The question, though, made it seem as if a trip to the Galapagos wasn't a $500 flight from the mainland, 700 miles from the coast, with its own multiday hotel and hostel and adventure logistics. It made it seem as if Ecuador has nothing else to offer—which is certainly does, from waves every day surf towns to rainforest adventures. There is plenty of Ecuador to appreciate outside of Darwin's coves. Of course, I am certain the Galapagos is a true must see, based on sixth-grade biology class and every guidebook. Maybe one day I will create an itinerary to see it, however, for now, our forty-five dollar day trip, via a forty-five-minute boat ride, that set sail thirty minutes from our coastal surf town would have to do.

We arrived at the island completely unprepared for the dusty mountainous tour. Our hostel day trip arranger, Jay, told us all about the great snacks aboard the vessel, particularly telling us about the delicious watermelon at least three times. We arrived in sandals and snorkel attire because Jay omitted the fact that, in addition to having an appetite, we also needed shoes for hiking. We would later learn that Jay was a huge stoner, which likely contributed to his snack-centric view of the trip.

In reality, the island tour was all about shit and boobies. As we shuffled uphill in our sandals, we learned that the island was located between the mainland of Ecuador and the actual Galapagos. It was a stopping point for the birds species, the booby, to rest, lay eggs, and shit. They shit on the sides of the mountains while in flight and they shit in perfect circles around their nests for protection. They shit where they wanted and they shit strategically. This island captured it all.

In particular, Isla de la Plata was famous for the wide variety of boobies that transit through it. There were brown-footed boobies, blue-footed boobies, yellow-footed boobies, and of course, our Ecuadorian tour guide's favorite, Peruvian boobies. The slights by our guide against Peru were restrained considering the rivalry between the two stems from repeated territorial disputes and wars. Deaths and battles meant that despite our guide's lighthearted jokes, the history of conflict between the countries was not exactly at the same level as a friendly college rivalry.

"Look at that loser couple," our tour guide pointed to a pair of boobies hiding in the brush with pale blue feet. Like a trip to the regular Galapagos, we learned about booby evolution and mating preferences. For example, the blue-footed boobies that have the bluest feet get the most attention from potential mates because the blue hue comes from a shrimpy sea creature they eat; the bluer the feet, the better hunter they must be. Our loser couple not only had pale feet, but also had not produced any eggs, contributing more to their loser category, according to the guide.

We also came across a nicely blue-footed mom and its giant baby with white feet. It made no sense that this baby bird was so giant, bigger than the mom, but the guide had no explanation. The guide was happy to have a small group of tourists who spoke English and we shared jokes in broken English and Spanish that made the German couple in our group continue to stare without any signs of amusement. In addition to providing his knowledge on boobies, the guide also provided a bit of Ecuadorian rap history by noting that we had to check out the 1998 song "El Gato Volador" (The Flying Cat) by El Chombo once we had a signal. It was quite the song.

Before we side stepped and slid in our sandals back down the hill to return to the boat, we saw the beautiful views of turquoise waves crashing on the dark brown rocks splattered with white. Although Darwin might have skipped over this place, it was still an experience worth at least $45.

Trips like this one kept me grounded and from thinking the world was only filled with bad people. I still mostly thought of the coastal locations in Ecuador in reference to which ones shipped the most cocaine or were home to the most bad guys, but at least the boobies allowed me to feel more in tune with nature for a few moments. The Agency gets in your head; I don't know whether it skews your perspective or just makes you unable to completely ignore the realities now apparent to you. It was more like the movies than I had realized.

CHAPTER 28

IT'S JUST LIKE THE MOVIES

It's hard to be part of the self-esteem generation that grew up with everyone getting a trophy. Now half the population is completely overconfident, and the other half is like, wait, am I actually good at anything? Or is everyone just telling me I'm good at things so that I stick around?

YOU'LL SEE IN BOTH James Bond and Jack Ryan that organizations like the Agency have a tendency to favor overly confident White men with limited foreign language capabilities. In that regard, working at the CIA is just like the movies. The preference for Georgetown University-educated men is ironic for an organization that aims to blend in with its surroundings. I'm not sure what screams *spy* more than a White guy walking around African countries in his boat shoes and khakis asking to speak with diplomats.

The Agency's mission of collecting intelligence from people is driven by human psychology and thus it is a self-aware organization, even if sometimes that awareness is delayed. Leaders are working to remedy the systemic biases around race. However, as in any organization, one error in the process can undo all improvements. The recruiters might engage with a variety of people, the interviewers might finally widen their scope of who has the potential to be successful in certain roles, and the home offices might finally be welcoming to all. However, what happens with the training cadre, who with their own biases, regularly fail multiple people of color? Later, executives at the top of the organization are wondering why they do not have good retention rates for people who aren't White.

The CIA is also just like the movies in its excellence. The jokes and the camaraderie among officers are the positive things that come from the pressure of powerful people around the globe actively listening to your analysis and expecting you not to be wrong. Within the US government, leaders expect the Agency to be able to accomplish anything in less than a week—from stopping fentanyl from coming into the US to answering thousands of detailed inquiries about potential terrorists wandering Europe.

If you didn't seem like you could cut it, people noticed.

"How do you think she made it through the hiring process?" I whispered to my friend and colleague, Christopher, after we both reviewed a poorly written report.

"She must speak Chinese," Christopher giggled, accurately identifying that sometimes the Agency was desperate enough for certain skills to probably see past other inadequacies. We arrogantly gossiped to boost our own confidence that we too deserved to be there.

The downside of extreme excellence is extreme imposter syndrome, essentially feeling like you are a fraud and are not good enough to be in the role that you have rightfully achieved. I thought I was the only one feeling like an imposter, as imposter syndrome tends to do, until I was in a leadership training course and a colleague of mine said, "every day I come into the office, I feel like an imposter."

This was a White man with a master's in economics and, as evidence of his overall acumen, he was a former Jeopardy contestant. I felt better for a second after he said this, thinking, "I'm not the only one who doesn't feel good enough," but then thought, "if this overqualified dude feels like he isn't good enough, then I don't stand a chance to ever feel good enough."

Imposter Syndrome is felt by most of those at the Agency who aren't complete narcissists, which might be a lower percentage compared to other organizations. The CIA has a thing for hiring operations officers who blur the line between arrogant and pathologically conceited. The confidence helps with the job they have of convincing foreigners to risk their livelihoods by telling the US their country's secrets. Analysts, the people aggregating the information that comes in from the field, deal with the historical pressure of predicting correctly whether a country will strike the US with missiles (Cuban Missile Crisis) or whether the US should expend millions of dollars in resources and manpower planning a raid that may or may not result in the capture of the terrorist responsible for the 9/11 attacks (Bin Laden). Even on a smaller scale, the predictions and outcomes are documented and briefed all over the US government. All parties are under pressure, of course, and that is part of the excitement of the job. The operations officer who is recruiting agents overcomes the pressure of being caught using careful planning, confidence, and often whiskey, while the analyst sweats it out in a tight pantsuit briefing the political people who drank too much coffee and are about to make potentially headline-making decisions.

Analysts are typically educated people who naturally question themselves in search of the right answer and then are further trained to question their already questioned conclusions.

"These structured analytic techniques help remove your assumptions based on your own past, your perspective, and your tendencies," the instructor began to explain how to set up the analysis of competing hypothesis technique that would help us reach conclusions based on an unbiased look at evidence.

"So," my colleague said, "we are here because we are intelligent, but we also cannot trust ourselves when we reach what we think is the answer?"

"Correct," the instructor responded.

Operations officers learned to use their gut instinct on the streets, while analysts were trained to question themselves at every inclination.

Operations officers often eventually function in tune with their instincts, working through doubts, while analysts' advanced training continues to revolve around doubting. Sometimes the doubting crossed into doubting their own capabilities.

For me, despite the increasing amount and complexity of information arriving to be analyzed, attempting to counter drug trafficking at its core remained a game of cat and mouse. Like other battles against bad actors, it evolved only when one side implemented new technology and the other had to adapt to the change. It was like if you took the aspect of the Tom and Jerry cartoon where one side (the drug traffickers) usually ended up the winners and mixed that cartoon with the *Groundhogs Day* movie in which each day/month/quarter/year became eerily similar. I was watching this type of *Tom and Jerry* on loop. Although the CIA did counternarcotics at a different level than the Joint Task Force I was at while in the Coast Guard, I was still getting tired of the same game. It did not help that new leadership had come in at the upper management level and overwhelmed my tolerance for bullshit that had already began to give me warning signals.

"Why is that guy in charge? He only stays awake in meetings if he is the one talking," one colleague said.

"Must be one of those people that just won't retire so they have to keep moving him around," another explained.

Not even the CIA is void of bureaucratic incompetence. However, the CIA is an organization of creating relationships, so I networked.

What office would be a good fit? What topic would allow me to improve my skills while taking a break from analyzing various aspects of cocaine movements toward the US?

I found something cool. Something that would take me up a level in strategy and keep me at a distance from reading about drugs and associated actors.

"Could I do it for a year? Like a rotation?" I asked the manager of the new office.

"Sure thing! Bring us what you know and then you can take the skills you learn here back down to your current office," he responded.

Perfect.

"Here's what it would look like," I explained a few options to my manager. "I could still do some work for this office, I would just be on a rotation to them. It would give me enough of a break to not get completely burned out and give you guys a connection to that office, plus I need a rotation anyways to get promoted," I said.

"Alright, let me see what the top tier says. To be honest, I do not think they are going to let you go."

"What?"

They did not let me go. Top management wanted to have some sort of hold on me to stick around since widespread disappointment in the new leadership had a lot of people leaving. Luckily, in my networking sprint I found an office of advanced analytics that was looking for someone who could take their high-flying ideas to be applied at the ground level. They offered me a rotation *or* full time change of office.

"I would love to do the rotation, but I'm not allowed to do a rotation because the office wants to keep me." I said to that manager. "I know I need a break, though, or I'm going to end up quitting it all and moving to a remote island."

In the usual irony of poor leadership, the attempt to forcefully hold me close caused me to remove myself from the office completely. They wouldn't give me the rotation, so I left my counterdrug position for a new permanent one in the advanced analytics office.

CHAPTER 29

SO HOW DO I GET OUT OF THIS ONE

I considered transitioning to the business world, but it was challenging to explain how my skills were relevant. I didn't have an MBA, but I had experience with supply chain. Supply chain disruption . . . specifically astute in the cocaine sector.

THE ONLY THING HARDER than getting *into* the CIA is *leaving* the CIA.

There comes a time when the privileges of the job are not enough to counter DC's high cost of living and its traffic problems. The two-hour traverse from the northwest to the southeast part of the city for happy hour becomes tiresome and buying a place big enough to fit two people and a kid (or dog) means you'll have a three-hour commute to work and will be living in a western Virginia town named after some Confederate. Some people make it happen. I loved my job and my colleagues, but I could not help but feel like I was no longer in the right place for *me*.

Trump and Pence were leading the country, and although I was proud of the CIA for continuing to speak truth to power, it was tiring.

"*What* is this?" After staying past ten the night before, my colleague, Jacqueline, had come in early to submit her formal response to a question about an intelligence article she wrote that had gone to the White House. A piece of paper was laid across her keyboard.

"No longer required!" she said as she read the note a manager had laid across her desk, which stated her analysis was no longer needed. Disheveled from coming in early, she dropped her purse under the desk and logged onto the computer without even taking off her jacket. "McMaster *resigned*?" I heard her dramatically wail over the cubical wall. McMaster had been the National Security Adviser who had asked the question about her article and, as of the submission of his resignation letter, he was no longer around to need the answer. "No one else wants this answer? Somebody has to care that I worked for seven hours to answer this single question. I spent seven hours collecting information, validating information, changing things back and forth based on management review, and formatting this long-ass response into five concise sentences in this stupid word doc with its stupid official formatting, but no one cares about the answer."

"Maybe you can still use the document toward your promotion," the woman across the cube had taken her headphones off to make an attempt to console Jacqueline. It wasn't about just McMaster though, but the general loss of consistency that happens when there is a 92 percent turnover of senior-level advisors in an administration, advisors that actively take into account the CIA's analysis. The government had paid Jacqueline overtime for an answer to a worthy question only for the administration's instability to waste those dollars, disregard the answer to a good question, and chip away at her sense of purpose.

One day, Vice President Mike Pence came to speak to CIA officers. This was after Trump had visited the CIA to incoherently speak about his votes and his inauguration crowd size in front of the CIA Memorial Wall that honors CIA employees who died in the line of service. His comments were tasteless at best,

You know, the military and the law enforcement, generally speaking, but all of it—but the military gave us tremendous percentages of votes. We were unbelievably successful in the election with getting the vote of the military. And probably almost everybody in this room voted for me, but I will not ask you to raise your hands if you did . . . And I was explaining about the numbers. We did a thing yesterday at the speech. Did everybody like the speech? I've been given good reviews. But we had a massive field of people. You saw them. Packed.

Pence arrived in an attempt to redeem the administration.

"Tomorrow's event: At noon The Vice President will be here to speak. Please arrive at 11:30 a.m. Do not arrive before 11:30 a.m., as you will be turned away from waiting," the email read.

"Reminder: Vice President Pence will be speaking at noon today. Arrive as early as 11:30 a.m. to claim your seat," the next email encouraged.

"It's time to come claim your seat for the Vice President's address to the CIA," at 11:45 a.m., the email tone changed from simply announcing to sounding slightly desperate for participants.

"Vice President is speaking momentarily! All officers are invited to come hear the Vice President," at 11:55 a.m., the poor person who was coordinating the event got real.

"*All,*" an instant message from upper office management flashed across the screen, "if you are not working on anything time sensitive, please go to the hall where the Vice President is speaking."

"Do you want to grab coffee?" My college behind my cube wall asked.

"Yeah, let's go for a walk," I responded.

Before locking my computer, another message came across, "Hey, team—relaying message from above. Please go to the hallway where the VP is speaking," the office manager passed along the request.

"Hey boss, you want any coffee?" we asked him.

"Nah I'm good, going to work on a few things here. I've got your promotion paperwork due in a few weeks," he said, clearly not doing anything time sensitive.

We walked upstairs to the coffee shop. It was packed. "Hey! Everyone, we really need people to come to this event, there are plenty of open seats!" An event coordinator was on a mission to get people in front of Mike Pence. "Are any of your employees available to attend?" she desperately asked the coffee shop's manager who motioned toward the long line of people waiting for coffee.

"No, thanks," a woman wearing a LGBTQ ally lanyard grabbed her latte and walked away. Others were equally disinterested. The coffee shop hummed with jazz music and the crowd did not even pretend they had anything more pressing to do.

"I remember when other presidents came, what an event!" my colleague reminisced about her fifteen plus years in the organization, "I've seen Bush and Obama!"

Pence, however, was different. Everyone had their own reason for avoiding the Pence event, for most of my office it was about respect for our colleagues. Pence had a reputation for actively working against the LGBTQ community, having voted against the *Don't Ask, Don't Tell* repeal in 2010 and supporting an amendment to Indiana's Constitution that would ban same-sex marriage. In 2018, he was the first vice president to give an address at the summit of a group known to be anti-LGBTQ. The administration also rejected the usual annual requests from US embassies to fly the rainbow pride flag on embassy flagpoles during LGBTQ Pride Month, despite the administration claiming to support the end of criminalization of homosexuality in nearly seventy countries that still outlaw it.

The CIA had come a long way in how they treated LGBTQ employees, historically preventing them from being hired and firing them upon being outed. They saw being gay as a vulnerability that could be used as blackmail against their officers. The organization eventually changed their tone and became the leading agency in supporting LGBTQ in the US government and military. If nothing else, their old views had caused them to lose skilled and valuable employees who represented the diversity in the world from which the CIA recruited agents to spy for them.

"This is so fun!" my operations officer colleague made another recruitment of an agent who would provide the CIA with information to support US security. "I feel like I'm in my twenties dating closeted married men who want to keep things on the down low," he reflected on the secrecy it took to meet up with agents who were providing information. "If I knew I could get paid for chatting up men in foreign countries and discretely planning follow-on dates, I would have applied to the CIA a lot earlier." Christopher was fluent in three languages, hilarious, and also gay. Despite the CIA's support for the LGBTQ community, he still occasionally struggled with revealing his whole self.

"I told my boss I needed to talk with my *partner* about the change in the overseas assignment," Christopher explained to me one day, "I keep avoiding saying *boyfriend* because I know he is really religious and in one of those gay-hating sects," Christopher stated as if it was routine to deal with these things. Then he continued with concern, "I really need him to advocate for me to keep my assignment, like he *has* to support it or I'm not going to be able to go. I can't risk having him know I'm gay and consciously or subconsciously deciding not to help me out!"

Before Christopher had his boyfriend, we would spend our lunch breaks gossiping about dating on the main floor near the coffee shop where nearly everyone would pass by at some point during their day. The big windows made the hallway feel open, like we were outside in the real world going on a walk to Starbucks, but the sun reflecting off the polished white floors was a reminder that we were still inside the immense and well-groomed CIA compound. Regardless of isolation from the outside world, it was a relief to come to this floor after working all morning in a windowless vaulted room.

"Oh, look at that, do you think he's fine?" Christopher motioned toward a young and fit man with blond and lightly gelled hair who was grabbing his coffee and thanking the barista with a dazzling smile. His crisp white dress shirt hugged his wide shoulders while his tight dress pants of the shorter style revealed playful rubber ducky patterned socks.

"Um, yes of course I think he's attractive. Plus, he has great style." I replied.

"You should say hi!" Christopher encouraged. "Just run into him or make a comment about lattes and giggle."

"Me? Why? What if he doesn't like me?" I asked.

"Well, that doesn't really matter. If he doesn't like you, then he is *bound* to like me!" Christopher cracked himself up, putting his palm to his chest to contain himself.

Christopher and I had a close friendship that naturally blossomed through our shared experiences starting a job at the CIA.

"When do you turn off your phone?" I asked him once.

"I leave it off my whole commute. The boys will just have to wait."

Vice President Pence was a reminder of those in power who actively worked against equal rights for people like Christopher, someone who is not only an amazing friend, but someone taking huge risks and sacrificing for our country.

The therapist asked me if I wanted kids, I told her I don't know. I always put myself in that category of women who didn't want kids: Oprah Winfrey, Jennifer Aniston, Casey Anthony . . .

I needed to clear my head from DC. I had just changed offices and was still not feeling settled. I tried surfing in Maryland on the weekends. When I could make the three-hour drive to get in the water, I felt refreshed. It was like with each session I went, I was becoming a new person. Or maybe I was washing away the messiness that had settled on the old one. *Was living in Montauk, New York really the last time I surfed regularly?* I was becoming renewed by going back to that old surfer girl still inside me and I knew that a six-hour round trip drive to get a piece of my soul back was not sustainable. I felt like my old self was coming back, only now I also could handle *most* of life's responsibilities and had skills and passions to contribute.

I still felt selfish for wanting more. I felt bad about leaving an organization that welcomed me and my flaws. It built me up to be a better and more aware person and here I was getting ready to say goodbye because I couldn't handle the lifestyle anymore. I had to accept, however, that the CIA supports our freedom as people of the United States, and it was time for me to exercise my own freedom to keep evolving into who I was and finding my place in the world.

Leaving the CIA behind is hard because in most job interviews, people want to hire you based on what have achieved in your previous positions. The CIA could not be more results oriented, however, the definition of covert action is "an activity or activities of the United States Government to influence political, economic, or military conditions abroad, where it is intended that *the role of the United States will not be apparent or acknowledged publicly."*

I wasted an Amazon hiring recruiter's time vaguely discussing the tasks I did at the CIA and then sharing the mollified result of my efforts.

"What were the results of you teaming with data scientists to create an application that tracked real time movements so that all analysts could access the information when needed?" the recruiter asked.

"Well, the result was that they could access the information and provide it to people in other countries when needed," I responded.

"But, what was the result?"

"We saved time? We increased our effectiveness?" I was struggling.

"Effectiveness doing what?"

"What we were trying to do," I gave up. I couldn't bring myself to say, "that's classified" like a total douche.

Trying not to talk about results made me sound like a teenager who went on an epic road trip with friends, then told his parents the car fuel tank was empty because he went to pick up groceries. While it was true that he went to pick up groceries as part of the road trip, he also did a ton of more interesting stuff that his parents were not allowed to know about. I tried a few more interviews, then pivoted to my real passion of continuing my education.

After studying for the graduate exams while I was at a low in Guantanamo, I could not ignore that something closer to my true passion was calling me. I had always wanted to work on a PhD. I considered it after undergraduate school, but was too confined by the demands of life, such as having a job that pays rent. I just was not ready. Another opportunity arose when I was leaving the Coast Guard. I managed to get one application into George Mason's Biodefense PhD program. The faculty were incredibly welcoming, but the rates of entry and high caliber of applications were not in my favor. The school's dean wrote the nicest rejection letter I had ever received.

You have a strong portfolio, and I can't point to any specific weakness. It simply is a matter of fierce competition for those three spots. Just to give you a general sense, our newly admitted students did their undergrad work at Brown, UVA, and Rutgers, averaged a 320 on the GRE, and had graduate degrees from Georgetown, Hopkins, etc. It is a very tough crowd.

I am convinced from your application, though, that you have what it takes to get a PhD. Have you applied to other programs?

My undergraduate work at California state schools did not make the cut, even with the rigor of their Friday morning surf classes. I was not mad about the dean of a school taking the time to explain why I was not accepted and encourage me to keep looking. Receiving the rejection at that point in life, directly after leaving the Coast Guard, also let me continue on to work in government and eventually be part of the CIA.

Not only did I get the chance to have a really cool job, but I learned what good leadership looks like. I basked in the presence of quality leaders at the Agency. Not all were great, but the worst at the CIA were nowhere close to the worst in the military. There were a lot of great ones.

"Yep, yep, just biking the afternoon away," the director of the directorate of operations was regularly down at the gym chatting it up with whoever had the gusto to say hello. He and his handlebar mustache pedaled away on the stationary bike as he winked at officers too shy to address him.

At an even higher level, when Director Gina Haspel was confirmed to lead the CIA, it was refreshing to see not only a woman, but someone who did not excel at public speaking take the helm and have the Agency's support. She had made it from the ground up, a skilled case officer who spent her career as far out of the spotlight as she could, now speaking in front of not only all of the organization but to the public for the Agency when needed as well. She had controversies attached to her career, but so did a lot of men in the CIA who still were given leadership opportunities.

At my level, the best manager told us to do our jobs well and he would handle the rest. "Listen, I've been in the Army, I've cleaned latrines, and I've gotten shot at. If someone here yells at me, I'm still going to go home to my family at the end of the day. Be as aggressive as you need to be. Don't worry about upper management; it's my job to handle them."

The CIA was not always the best functioning organization, but it had people who knew there was a better way and did their best to implement it. It had its complainers, but the majority had an adaptive mindset. Things got reorganized once and most of the old cowboys despised the changes, but the young fresh faces who lived in a world with constant changes overcame the structural adjustments. The CIA welcomed and supported their new employee's flexibility and optimism by providing incredible developmental opportunities like training, education, and travel.

Of course, treating people well was not *only* because the CIA was a quality organization. It cannot be ignored that its motives for a happy workforce lie in not wanting disgruntled employees to sell off the Agency's secrets to the highest foreign bidder. Still, the dedication to its people was something to be admired.

As I looked for a way out, I was intrigued by the University of San Diego's Leadership Studies course. It reminded me of the master's in Homeland Security that I did through Penn State while I was enlisted. Leadership Studies was a vague new topic, like Homeland Security, but I hoped that like Homeland Security, Leadership Studies would eventually be an area of focus that I did not have to overly explain. Prior to 2020, I would tell someone in a job interview that my final paper at Penn State was on preparedness for pandemics, specifically concerning non-illness absenteeism among healthcare workers — what might cause them to not show up to work and how hospitals could better support their needs during a pandemic.

"Pandemics? What is there to study?" I was nicely admired for completing a master's, but rarely was what I studied seen as relevant. Once the worldwide coronavirus pandemic hit, I sighed in relief that I would no longer have to fully explain pandemic risk and the importance of hospital workers in those types of crises.

San Diego's wave-filled coastline did not hurt the program's appeal. I visited twice just to make sure it was going to be a good fit. During these visits I began to awkwardly reveal to those that asked that I was an analyst at the CIA looking to pivot my career. In DC, I could rarely get myself to say CIA, since the advice for casual conversations was to avoid the topic, mention something about boring government work, and change the subject. The tours of the University of San Diego became my practicing grounds.

"CIA! Interesting! Am I allowed to ask what you did there?" the professor responded.

"Uh, yes, you can ask anything I guess. I'll just have to tell you if I can't exactly respond," I replied. I had just managed to say I worked at the CIA but was stumbling through the follow up questions. The application for the school itself became another obstacle. I had to wait for approval of my resume, statement of purpose, and figure out who at the Agency would be allowed to openly write a letter of recommendation.

CHAPTER 30

THAT'S A WRAP

The rat race is funny because you might think you're avoiding it,
but you've only transferred yourself to another racetrack.

BY FEBRUARY 2020, I was starting to get responses to my applications. While I was not successful in many of the more traditional PhD programs, the University of San Diego welcomed me with open arms. Maybe the traditional programs knew that I was not in a place where I should be dedicating all my free hours to being a professor's indentured servant. Or maybe they thought my resume was a total lie. As the years added up, more important than a PhD has been the time to rest, recover, and reflect. I avoided the nine to five rat race for ten years. By eluding that, I also avoided stability, or looked for it in the wrong place.

"How was the weekend?" my cubical mate at the CIA asked per the usual Monday morning routine.

"Good, yours?" I managed to lift my lips into a slight smile. I knew from glancing in the bathroom mirror that morning that I was more pale than usual. I had undergone an abortion on Friday night and decided to go into work still bleeding on Monday morning. The relationship that led to this situation should have ended six months prior, but it didn't end until a few months from that moment. A year later, I took time to reflect. *Why didn't I take more days off from work? Why did I write that Casey Anthony joke?* I had a few regrets about it, but overall, I felt grateful that I didn't have to frantically travel or fly anywhere to start the process as soon as possible (even with my early paranoia, the pregnancy wasn't confirmed until after week four). Because the clinic was nearby, I was able to delay the procedure for a day so that I could really think about my situation and feel what was happening. It was a balance of making a decision quickly, but not too quickly. Having the time to consider what I was doing changed *me*, even if it didn't change my decision.

In pondering what my life had become, I found the humor between the lines of darkness and was ready to begin to confront the darkness that lingers between expressions of humor. I still do not know what I am doing with this leadership degree. Getting into politics would have been a noble option if I did not have so many nudes floating around through various area codes . . . and possibly country codes. I am grateful I have the GI Bill to finally help me make the transition to another line of work, but I have days where I doubt my ability to find a job, let alone find something I really want to do. It feels like I am leaving the Coast Guard again, only this time I do not have a government job ready to take me as I am and make me into what they need. I am just me, without a clear path, other than attending classes and making the most out of the experience. It scares me because I think of the lieutenant who killed himself because he could not see a path outside of his regimented environment.

I wish I had better lessons and a strong passion for the future with which I could close out the stories. This whole book is an accumulation of wading through rough waters that I willingly jumped into or were part of the circumstances. It is an ongoing series of challenges that were softened by going through them with caring and funny people who continue to make it all tolerable. I guess my biggest hope is that I can look back on the last few chapters with as much humor as I could with the first ones. It is easier to lead when you don't care what happens to you and your goal is just to make sure the people who you are leading end up better off than you are.

By being in San Diego, I have found some hope and faith again through surfing. The slow sunrise over the water, from dark to light blue, then to pastels over Ocean Beach's sometimes brutal surf conditions has strengthened my *trust in life* mental muscles that I found had become quite weak from training, travel, and struggling with what I could control. Occasionally now, a wave will hold me under, but so far, it always brings me back up. It has given me another chance to drop in on a nice right, make a sweeping bottom turn, cut back down, and decide how I want to ride the rest.

Some weeks, I overdo the surfing and have to come back to moderation. I have to remind myself that I am not stuck at an isolated unit on the end of Long Island. An overextended escape from land to sea is no longer an adaption to avoid a toxic environment, but it is me avoiding addressing what those experiences have led to internally. Achievements, movement, and career success can hide pain that is inside of us.

Some days are still not easy. I still cannot discuss much of what I did at the Agency, the work I am most proud of, the details of my travels, and the people who have impacted me. Sometimes I feel like that part of me leaves me, as if those experiences never even happened, as if all I have are the chaotic Coast Guard experiences.

In my dreams though, I am back to the sand dunes, watching nature wake up, watching how my friends have learned to live a little better as they skateboard around with me in the dark. I am lucky I have found the chance to get back on a path more genuine to me.

ACKNOWLEDGMENTS

THANKS TO THE ARMED Service Arts Partnership founder and team members for enabling such an amazing organization that put me on the path to writing this book. Thanks also to friends and family who got me through this journey: Anastasia Hannebrink, Meg Antonczyk, Tahina Montoya, Janeth Del Cid, Amanda Garcia, Katie Walsh, Jeremy Lopez, Charity King, Clara Gonzalez, Lauren Efman, Diego Malvar, Lynette Pettinicchi, Kim and Colby Buchanan, Becky Wyckoff, Ed, Corey, Brandon, PSU 305's logistics team, Mel, Julia, plus all of those I cannot name or who I renamed for these stories, especially all my Kent School classmates and the instructor cadre—you all are the best.

Also, thanks to my editor Howard Lovy, who helped me give voice to my experiences.

CPSIA information can be obtained
at www.ICGtesting.com
Printed in the USA
JSHW020637160623
43319JS00004B/14